Clive Hamilton is the author of *Growth Fetish* and Executive Director of the Australia Institute, Australia's foremost public interest think tank. Described as 'Australia's most amazing economist', he has held visiting positions at the Australian National University, the University of Sydney and the University of Cambridge.

Richard Denniss is Deputy Director of the Australia Institute. He has taught economics at the University of Newcastle, was Chief of Staff to Senator Natasha Stott Despoja and has published widely on the impact of government policy on society and the environment.

Af-flu-en-za (n). 1. The bloated, sluggish and unfulfilled feeling that results from efforts to keep up with the Joneses. 2. An epidemic of stress, overwork, waste and indebtedness caused by dogged pursuit of the Australian dream. 3. An unsustainable addiction to economic growth.

FROM THE BEST-SELLING AUTHOR OF *GROWTH FETISH*

AFFLUENZA

WHEN TOO MUCH IS NEVER ENOUGH

CLIVE HAMILTON
and RICHARD DENNISS

ALLEN&UNWIN

First published in 2005

Copyright © Clive Hamilton and Richard Denniss 2005

Allen & Unwin
83 Alexander Street
Crows Nest NSW 2065
Australia
Phone: (61 2) 8425 0100
Fax: (61 2) 9906 2218
Email: info@allenandunwin.com
Web: www.allenandunwin.com

National Library of Australia
Cataloguing-in-Publication entry:

Hamilton, Clive.
    Affluenza: when too much is never enough.

    Includes index
    ISBN 978 1 74114 671 4
    ISBN 1 74114 671 2.

    1. Consumer behaviour. 2. Consumption (Economics) – Moral
    and ethical aspects. 3. Materialism – Psychological
    aspects. 4. Quality of life. 5. Work and family. I.
    Denniss, Richard. II. Title.

303.4

Set in 11/14.5 Adobe Garamond by Midland Typesetters, Victoria, Australia
Printed in Australia by McPherson's Printing Group

10 9 8 7

CONTENTS

Preface

The meaning of life has tantalised philosophers for centuries, yet in recent years Australians have been acting as though they have found the answer—to own a big house and receive a \$10 000 pay rise. Despite public endorsement of this belief, in quieter moments most of us would admit that we need much more if we are to live a fulfilling life.

This book poses one simple question: if the economy has been doing so well, why are we not becoming happier? In seeking an answer, we look at how Australians live, work and consume. We describe how corporations, advertisers, the media and politicians operate to ensure that Australians are always thinking about what they lack, rather than using the opportunities our wealth presents for living rich lives and building a better society.

Although this is a book about the sicknesses of affluence, it does not argue that we would be better off poor. Instead, the proposition is that only by recognising our material abundance can we begin the task of improving the other aspects of our lives—

our families, our communities, the natural environment and our minds.

In 2003 Allen & Unwin published Clive Hamilton's *Growth Fetish*, which has since been published around the world. *Affluenza* takes the growth fetish argument further, exploring how the phenomenon pervades every sphere of life. *Growth Fetish* was aimed at an international audience, whereas *Affluenza* is about Australia, examining how materialism and money hunger have changed our culture and shaped our politics. This book doesn't stop at analysing Australia's malaise. Karl Marx once wrote, 'The philosophers have only interpreted the world, in various ways; the point, however, is to change it'. To this end, the concluding chapters seek to answer the question: What is the alternative?

Acknowledgments

This book draws on papers produced by The Australia Institute, a public-interest think-tank based in Canberra <www.tai.org.au>. We are indebted to Christie Breakspear and Liz Mail, co-authors of two of those papers. We also draw on research the Institute commissioned from outside experts, especially Barbara Pocock, Jane Clarke, Michael Flood and Richard Eckersley.

Claire Barbato, Alex Walton and Leigh Thomas provided valuable research and editorial assistance. Elizabeth Weiss at Allen & Unwin provided helpful guidance, and Chris Pirie expertly edited the manuscript. Of course, all opinions expressed in the book are those of the authors.

Part One

A SOCIETY GOING NOWHERE

Chapter 1

What is affluenza?

*Af-flu-en-za n. 1. The bloated, sluggish and
unfulfilled feeling that results from efforts to keep
up with the Joneses. 2. An epidemic of stress,
overwork, waste and indebtedness caused by dogged
pursuit of the Australian dream. 3. An unsustainable
addiction to economic growth.*[1]

Wanting

In 2004 the Australian economy grew by over $25 billion, yet
the tenor of public debate suggests that the country is in a dire
situation. We are repeatedly told of funding shortages for hospitals, schools, universities and public transport, and politicians
constantly appeal to that icon of Australian spirit, the 'Aussie
battler'. Political rhetoric and social commentary continue to
emphasise deprivation—as if we are living in the nineteenth
century and the problems facing the country have arisen because
we are not rich enough.

When the Labor Party lost the federal election in 2004 it
declared that, like the conservatives, it must pay more attention
to growth and the economy. It would seem that achieving an
economic growth rate of 4 per cent is the magic potion to cure all
our ills. But how rich do we have to be before we are no longer a
nation of battlers? Australia's GDP has doubled since 1980; at

a growth rate of 3 per cent, it will double again in 23 years and quadruple 23 years after that. Will our problems be solved then? Or will the relentless emphasis on economic growth and higher incomes simply make us feel more dissatisfied?

In the private domain, Australia is beset by a constant rumble of complaint—as if we are experiencing hard times. When asked whether they can afford to buy everything they really need, nearly two-thirds of Australians say 'no'. If we remember that Australia is one of the world's richest countries and that Australians today have real incomes three times higher than in 1950, it is remarkable that such a high proportion feel so deprived. Average earnings exceed $50 000 a year, yet a substantial majority of Australians who experience no real hardship—and indeed live lives of abundance—believe that they have difficulty making ends meet and that they qualify as battlers.

In the coming decade most of our income growth will be spent on consumer products the craving for which has yet to be created by advertisers. Our public concerns might be about health and the environment, but our private spending patterns show that the majority of Australians feel they suffer from a chronic lack of 'stuff'. The problem is that after we have renewed our stuff yet again, there is not enough money left to fund investments in hospitals and schools. We want better public services but seem unwilling to forgo more income in the form of taxes to pay for those services. Australia does not have a public health funding crisis: it has a flat-screen TV crisis.

It wasn't meant to be this way. Nineteenth century economists predicted that the abundance made possible by technological advance and the modern organisation of work would result in the emergence of 'post-materialist' humans—people existing on a higher plane, where their cultural, intellectual and spiritual powers are refined. In such a world the importance of economic considerations would naturally diminish. The 1960s and 1970s saw a flood of literature predicting a future in which technological progress would allow for us to work only a few hours a week and our main problem would be how best to enjoy our leisure. Futurists saw a society transformed by the fruits of sustained growth—a society in which humankind, freed of the chore of making a living, would devote itself to activities that are truly fulfilling.

But, instead of witnessing the end of economics, we live in a time when economics and its concerns are more dominant than ever before. Instead of our growing wealth freeing us of our materialist preoccupations, it seems to have had the opposite effect. People in affluent countries are now even more obsessed with money and material acquisition, and the richer they are the more this seems to be the case.

As a rule, no matter how much money people have they feel they need more. Why else would people in rich countries such as Australia keep striving to become richer, often at the expense of their own happiness and that of their families? Even the mega-rich seem unable to accept that they have all they need, always comparing themselves unfavourably with their neighbours. Most people cling to the belief that more money means more happiness. Yet when they reach the financial goals they have set they find they do not feel happier—except perhaps fleetingly. Rather than question the whole project, they engage in an internal dialogue that goes like this:

> I hoped that getting to this income level would make me feel contented. I do have more stuff, but it doesn't seem to have

done the trick. I obviously need to set my goals higher. I'm sure
I'll be happy when I'm earning an extra $10 000 because then
I'll be able to buy the other things I want.

Of course, raising the threshold of desire in this way creates an
endless cycle of self-deception: like the horizon, our desires always
seem to stay ahead of where we are. This cycle of hope and disappointment lies at the heart of consumer capitalism.

Our own achievements are never enough in a society like this.
As Gore Vidal said, 'Whenever a friend succeeds, a little something
in me dies'. Even if we do come out in front of our peers, the chances
are we will start to compare ourselves with those on the next rung of
the ladder. Our new discontent causes us to set our goals higher
still. In a world dominated by money hunger, if our expectations
continue to rise in advance of our incomes we will never achieve a
level of income that satisfies. Richard Easterlin, who did much of the
early work in this field, described this phenomenon as a 'hedonic
treadmill', where people have to keep running in order to keep up
with the others but never advance. The only way to win is to stop
playing the game.

Rich societies such as Australia seem to be in the grip of a collective psychological disorder. We react with alarm and sympathy
when we come across an anorexic who is convinced she is fat,
whose view of reality is so obviously distorted. Yet, as a society
surrounded by affluence, we indulge in the illusion that we are
deprived. Despite the obvious failure of the continued accumulation of material things to make us happy, we appear unable to
change our behaviour. We have grown fat but we persist in the
belief that we are thin and must consume more. Perhaps we blind
ourselves to the facts; perhaps the cure seems more frightening

than the disease; or perhaps we just don't know there is an alternative. For these reasons the epidemic of overconsumption that pervades rich societies has been dubbed 'affluenza'.[2] Psychotherapist and 'affluenza authority' Jessie H. O'Neill has provided a 'clinical definition' of the condition:

> The collective addictions, character flaws, psychological wounds, neuroses, and behavioral disorders caused or exacerbated by the presence of, or desire for money/wealth . . . In individuals, it takes the form of a dysfunctional or unhealthy relationship with money, regardless of one's socio-economic level. It manifests as behaviors resulting from a preoccupation with—or imbalance around—the money in our lives.

Affluenza describes a condition in which we are confused about what it takes to live a worthwhile life. Part of this confusion is a failure to distinguish between what we want and what we need. In 1973, 20 per cent of Americans said a second car was a 'necessity'; by 1996 the figure had risen to 37 per cent.[3] Among other items that have become necessities in most Australian homes in recent years are plasma-screen TVs, air conditioning, personal computers, second bathrooms, mobile phones and, increasingly, private health insurance and private schooling for children.

Neoliberal economic policies have set out to promote higher consumption as the road to a better society. All the market-based reforms in the last two decades have been predicated on the belief that the best way to advance Australia's interests is to maximise the growth of income and consumption. No one has dared to criticise this. But the rapid expansion of consumption has imposed high costs, on the overconsumers themselves, on society and on the natural environment, as discussed in the following chapters. In addition to the rapid increase in consumer debt, higher levels of consumption are driving many Australians to work themselves sick. Yet our desire for various commodities (larger houses, sophisticated home appliances, expensive personal items, and so on) is continually recreated—an illness that entered a particularly virulent phase in the 1990s with the trend described as 'luxury fever'.

Luxury fever

Popular folklore has always held a fascination with the profligate lifestyles of the monied classes. Sociologists have analysed how extravagance serves as a device whereby the rich differentiate themselves from the mass of the population. One of the earliest commentators on this was Thorstein Veblen, who coined the phrase 'conspicuous consumption' in his 1899 book *The Theory of the Leisure Class*. For their part, the masses watch the behaviour of the rich with a mixture of awe, envy and scorn. This attraction is the reason for the continuing popularity of magazines, newspapers and, more recently, television shows that expose the lifestyles of the rich and famous.

The sustained growth of the Australian economy in the postwar period elevated the bulk of the working class to income levels that were typical of the middle class of a previous generation. The boundaries between the consumption patterns of the middle and working classes began to blur, and it became increasingly difficult to separate their financial, educational and social aspirations. Surveys in which respondents were asked to define their social position have shown fewer and fewer people willing to identify themselves as working class. Indeed, 93 per cent of Australians believe they are in the middle-income bracket (that is, the middle 60 per cent) and only 6.4 per cent see themselves in the bottom 20 per cent and 0.7 per cent in the top 20 per cent.[4] The consequence of this merging of classes and the confusion about the incomes of others is that emulation of the spending and consumption habits of the wealthy, which was once confined to the upper levels of the middle class, now characterises Australian society.

The collapse of the demarcation between the rich, the middle class and the poor is associated with the scaling-up of desire for prestige brands and luxury styles of particular goods. Even people on modest incomes aspire to Luis Vuitton—if not the handbag, at least the T-shirt. We have witnessed an across-the-board escalation of lifestyle expectations. The typical household's desired standard of living is now so far above the actual standard afforded by the average income that people feel deprived of the 'good life'. Television and magazines play a crucial role in this racheting-up process, not so much through advertising but more through presenting opulence as normal and attainable.

So, although ordinary citizens have always eyed and envied the rich, in affluent countries in the past two decades a qualitative change has occurred in the relationship. In *Luxury Fever* Robert Frank noted that spending on luxury goods in the United States had been growing four times faster than spending overall.[5] The 'new luxury' market is said to be increasing by 10–15 per cent a year, far outpacing the growth of the economy in general.[6] This is reflected in booming sales of luxury travel, luxury cars, pleasure craft, cosmetic surgery, trophy homes, holiday homes and profes-sional-quality home appliances. The 'democratisation of luxury' has undermined the positional signalling of many goods pre-viously reserved for the very rich—a trend due partly to rising incomes and partly to the marketing strategies of the makers of luxury brands, which include the introduction of entry-level products in order to increase market share.[7] The argument is made pithily in a 2004 advertisement for a car. Next to the bold declaration 'LUXURY HAS ITS PRICE. (How does $39 990 sound?)', it states, 'There was a time when luxury was a different thing, stuffy, old and unaffordable. That time has gone . . .'[8]

This suggests a new distinction between the specialised luxury consumption that is confined to the mega-rich and the forms of luxury consumption characteristic of the bulk of the population. Of course, the luxury spending of the mega-rich sets a benchmark for the general populace, a benchmark that must, by its nature, keep rising in order to remain out of reach of all but the few. This requires continued creativity on the part of the mega-rich and on the part of those who supply them. The boom in sales of luxury cars—sales have more than doubled since 1993[9]—is depriving the mega-rich of their exclusivity. In response, the prestige car makers are now offering vehicles made to order and costing up to $1 million, thereby exclud-ing the ordinary rich and the middle class.

The changing symbolism of credit cards plots the path of luxury fever. Ten years ago the gold credit card was a mark of distinction, a sign that you had made it—or at least that was the message the credit card companies put out. But too many people began to qualify for the gold card and its symbolic value became diluted. So the credit card companies invented the platinum card, designed to be accessible only to those at the very top of the pile. Crucially, the platinum card was kept out of the hands of the general public: you could get one only if your bank wrote to you and offered it, and for that you needed, at a minimum, an income stretching to six figures. The mystery surrounding the platinum card added to its allure. This was a quiet symbol of superiority. It is a strange test of status: extraordinary talent won't get you one; a superior education means nothing; decades of service to the community or exceptional moral character are of no account. All you need to qualify for this status symbol is a bucket of money, acquired by fair means or foul.

And what does the owner of a platinum credit card get, apart from a very high credit limit? One bank tells its clientele that its Platinum Visa card 'is the ultimate choice for those who demand benefits and rewards that match their lifestyle. Powerful credit limits, prestige services and distinctive privileges combine to deliver exceptional levels of personal recognition'.[10] The owners of this card can luxuriate in access to a personal concierge service available 24 hours a day. The American Express Platinum card comes with a dedicated team of service professionals:

> For those times when you need assistance with life's little demands, Platinum Concierge is there for you, whenever and wherever you need it. There are times a birthday is mentioned to you a moment before it's belated. Or perhaps your anniversary is just around the corner. Simply call upon your Concierge to organise a speedy bouquet and a reservation at the finest restaurant.[11]

The card appears to be for people who neglect their families: 'No more milling about in queues, let us do the running around for you so you have more time to do the things that matter most'. Naturally, the things that matter most are concerned with making more money, rather than returning the love and care of those close to you. One commentator missed the point when he observed, 'Whether people really need some of the services is questionable . . . It's not that hard to make your own reservation or order flowers'.[12]

In 2004 the Commonwealth Bank spoilt the party by lowering the bar for a platinum card and allowing *anyone* to apply for one. Imagine that—'platinum for the people'. Determined to stay ahead of the game, American Express has now introduced a black credit card known as the Centurion. This card promises a 'six-star life experience' and 'access to the inaccessible'. One Centurion card owner called on the concierge service in Australia to return an Armani suit for alterations to the shop in Milan where he had bought it; another sent the concierge off to Taiwan to buy some out-of-print books.[13] An envious platinum card holder breathlessly emailed:

> Regarding the AMEX Centurion, I was at a friend's place on Saturday night and he received the card Friday. It comes in the most unbelievable package—solid wood (maybe cedar) box lined with velvet.
>
> He didn't request the card, just a letter from Auspost saying that he had a package to pick up.[14]

There is a pathos about this desire for the symbols of status, one that seems to reflect a need to be loved and admired.[15] This is what the luxury fever gripping Australia reveals us to be—a nation of consumers desperately seeking acknowledgment and admiration. Having discarded the verities of a previous era, standards that, for all their faults, at least gave us a sense of who we were and how we fitted into society, we now float in a sea of ambiguity and insecurity.

Buying an identity

Some psychologists argue that our actions are driven by a desire for 'self-completion', the theory being that we seek to bring our actual self into accord with our ideal self, or who we wish to be.[16] Today, almost all buying is to some degree an attempt to create or renew a concept of self. We complete ourselves symbolically by acquiring things that compensate for our perceived shortcomings. A vast marketing infrastructure has developed to help us manufacture ideal selves and to supply the goods to fill the gap between the actual and the ideal. The marketers understand much better than we do how we want to create an ideal self. As the CEO of Gucci says, 'Luxury brands are more than the goods. The goods are secondary because first of all you buy into a brand, then you buy the products. They give people the opportunity to live a dream'.[17] It is fair to assume that this dream is not the same as the one had by Martin Luther King.

Because it acts as the interface between the self and the world, clothing is perfect for providing the bridge between who we actually are and who we want to be seen to be. Cars and houses do the same, because people look at us 'through' our cars and houses.

In modern Australia the gap between our actual and ideal selves is widening. We are urged to aspire to a better, slimmer, richer, more sophisticated ideal self, and that ideal self is increasingly an exterior one. More than at any other time we feel the eyes of the world on us. This is the source of a longing to be something other than we are—something other than we can be. Perhaps this is why the increasing level of materialism that characterises affluent societies has been shown to be associated with declining wellbeing and a rise in pathological behaviours. American psychologist Tim Kasser summarises a decade of research into the relationship between materialistic values and our sense of security, our feelings of self-worth and the quality of our relationships:

> Materialistic values are both a symptom of an underlying insecurity and a coping strategy taken on in an attempt to alleviate problems and satisfy needs . . . The arguments and data . . . show that successfully pursuing materialistic goals fails to increase one's happiness. When people and nations make progress in their materialistic ambitions, they may experience some temporary improvement of mood, but it is likely to be short-lived and superficial.
>
> Materialistic values of wealth, status and image work against close interpersonal relationships and connection to others, two hallmarks of psychological health and high quality of life.[18]

These research results, which serve only to confirm centuries of folk wisdom, have begun to be replicated in Australian studies.[19] The evidence points to the conclusion that the more materialistic we become the more we try to cope with our insecurities through consuming, and the less contented we are. It also suggests that more materialism means poorer relationships.

Despite the barrage of advertising that tries to tell us otherwise, the more materialistic we are the less free we are. Why? Because we must commit more of our lives to working to pay for our material desires. And the more acquisitive we are the more our desires and the means of satisfying them are determined by others. Acquisitive people derive their sense of identity and their imagined place in society from the things they own, yet the symbols that confer that self-worth and status are at the whim of external forces—of fashion. Materialism thus robs us of autonomy.[20]

We have no trouble recognising that excessive alcohol consumption and excessive gambling harm the people concerned as well as those around them. Yet shopping can also be a response to obsessive or addictive behaviour. Psychologists have recently identified a pathological condition known as 'oniomania', or 'compulsive shopping', defined as an obsessive-compulsive disorder characterised by a preoccupation with shopping experienced as irresistable and resulting in frequent and excessive buying. People with oniomania find their shopping is out of control; they buy more than they need, often setting out to buy one or two items but coming home with bags full of things they could not resist. They often spend more than they can afford and rack up debts that build until a crisis occurs. After shopping binges they are visited by feelings of regret. If this sounds like the experience of almost everyone, then that is no more than the theme of this book, and the psychiatrists have merely identified the more extreme form of a widespread social condition.

Compulsive shopping has been called the 'smiled upon' addiction because it is socially sanctioned. But its consequences can be far-reaching. It often results in financial hardship, distress and family difficulties. Psychologists have also noticed some interesting patterns of co-morbidity, that is, the simultaneous presence of other disorders. Individuals afflicted by oniomania often suffer from eating disorders, drug dependence, and other impulse-control disorders such as anorexia among women and gambling among men.[21] The research shows that most compulsive buyers have histories of depression, anxiety disorders and substance abuse. Yet 'shopping til you drop' is seen as the sign of a happy-go-lucky disposition rather than a meaningless life.

Like alcohol, shopping has become both an expression of our discontent and an apparent cure for it. Indeed, it has recently been shown that oniomania can be treated effectively with particular antidepressant drugs,[22] suggesting that the condition is not in itself a psychological disorder but rather a manifestation of something more pervasive—entrenched depression and anxiety for which shopping is a form of self-medication, a phenomenon widely acknowledged in the expression 'retail therapy'.

Must we wear hairshirts?

Some readers might accuse us of being too harsh, too judgmental, perhaps a touch Calvinistic. Why shouldn't Australians enjoy the fruits of their labour? What's wrong with a bit of luxury? Isn't it reasonable to want to build some financial security? The answer to these questions is of course 'yes'. We are not arguing that we should build humpies and live in self-satisfied deprivation. That would be to completely misconstrue the argument of this book. It is not money and material possessions that are the root of the problem: it is our *attachment* to them and the way they condition our thinking, give us our self-definition and rule our lives.

The problem is not that people own things: the problem is that things own people. It is not consuming but consumerism we criticise; not affluence but affluenza. The signs are easy to see in others—the subtle and not-so-subtle displays of wealth, the one-upmanship, the self-doubt—and most Australians acknowledge that our society is too materialistic and money driven. But it is much harder to recognise and admit to the signs in ourselves because that can be confronting. So our claim that the answer lies in detachment rather than denial has more in common with Buddhism than with Calvinism. We argue that the obsessive pursuit of more and more fails to make us happy and that in pursuit people often sacrifice the things that really can make them happier.

There is, of course, a trap in the distinction between having money and being attached to money: it is easy to convince ourselves that, apart from a few special things, we can take or leave our possessions. Many wealthy people grow tired of being defined by their wealth and convince themselves they could do perfectly well without it. And most of us, at times, fantasise about living a simpler life, unencumbered by 'stuff'. Until we test ourselves, though, these are just comforting stories. This is why the emerging group of downshifters—people who have voluntarily reduced their income—is so important. Each downshifter has, so to speak, put their money where their mouth is.

The defenders of consumerism—the advertisers and the neoliberal commentators, think-tankers and politicians—repeat the comforting stories. It's good to aspire to own your own home, surround yourself with nice things, look after the needs of your children, and save for your retirement. Yes, we are lucky that in a rich country such as Australia many of us can do these things, but most people reach a point in their lives, some at eighteen and some at 88, when they ask, 'Work, buy, consume, die: is that all there is?' Each time someone asks such a question the market shudders, because if there is more to life than earning and consuming the odds are that when people realise it they will devote less time to paid work and consume less.

In writing about affluenza in Australia we do not deny that poverty remains. We are, however, saying that material deprivation is not the dominant feature of life in Australia. Affluence is. It helps no one to exaggerate the extent of poverty: that simply reinforces the curious but widespread belief that most people are struggling. If the majority of people can't afford to buy everything they really need, why should we be particularly concerned with the poor? And the bigger the problem seems the less likely the populace is willing to believe that something can be done about it.

We argue that, to tackle the problem of poverty, we must first tackle the problem of affluence. And the problem with affluence is that once people become affluent they continue to believe that more money is the key to a happier life when the evidence suggests that it makes no difference beyond a certain threshold. This belief has powerful personal and social ramifications, not the least being that the affluent become more preoccupied with themselves. That is why Australians are richer than ever but less inclined to sympathise with the dispossessed. So conservative politicians and radio shock jocks vilify the poor. Consumerism and growth fetishism have become the enemies of a fairer Australia.

Chapter 2
Consuming passions

*In rich countries today, consumption consists of
people spending money they don't have to buy goods
they don't need to impress people they don't like.*

——anon

Australians have been on a decade-long consumption binge
fuelled by the extraordinary growth in consumer credit and
home loans. In this we are following the United States, where,
as one estimate puts it, luxury spending grew by 28 per cent
in the first half of 2004 alone.[1] Luxury consumption is hard
to track systematically because most luxury goods today are
merely specialised versions of normal goods, rather than specific
items that can be separately identified. Official statistics do
not differentiate between gold-plated bathroom fittings and
stainless steel ones, luxury yachts and tinnies, boutique ales
and standard beers, vacations in five-star resorts and holidays
in fibro shacks. Investing normal goods with the perceptions
of exclusivity and status is an essential element of 'luxury
fever'. It is not hard, though, to paint a picture of the extent
and nature of overconsumption. So, what have Australians been
splashing out on?

Our houses

The primary target of excessive consumption spending in Australia is undoubtedly the home. Houses are bigger than ever, with more bedrooms and bathrooms and filled with more luxurious fittings and appliances. Australians want to live in homes with more space than the residents can actually use. Between 1985 and 2000 the average floor area of new houses increased by 31 per cent, from 170 square metres to 221 square metres, and the size of apartments increased by 25 per cent, to an average of 139 square metres.[2] In the mid-1950s the average size of new houses was about 115 square metres, that is, half the size of houses today (see Figure 1). Many new houses now have three-car garages that measure 50 square metres. According to the national marketing manager for A.V. Jennings, 'It's the great Australian dream: people will build the houses they can afford'. With the average mortgage for new homebuyers growing by more than 70 per cent in the ten years to 2001,[3] it would be more accurate to say that people will build the houses they cannot afford.

This expansion in the size of houses has been occurring at a time when the average number of people in each household is shrinking. In 1955 each household had an average of 3.6 people; by 1970 it had fallen to 3.3 people and by 2000 it had reached only 2.6 people (see Figure 1). Put another way, in 1970 an average new house had 40 square metres of floor space for each occupant, whereas today each occupant has 85 square metres. The number of bedrooms per dwelling has increased from 0.82 for each occupant in 1970 to 1.15 today. No wonder house prices have risen so dramatically.

Bigger houses and more space for each occupant are changing the way we interact. When children go to separate rooms to watch

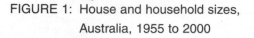

FIGURE 1: House and household sizes,
Australia, 1955 to 2000

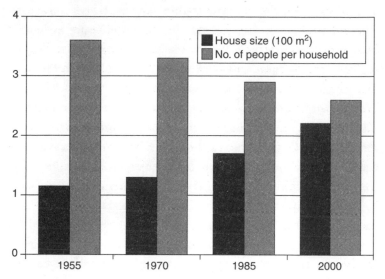

their own television sets, not only do parents have less control over what the children view and how much time they spend in front of the box: they are also not around to provide context for and commentary on what their children see. Nor do children learn to negotiate with others over how to share space in the house. In the case of couples without children, he and she can occupy separate sections of the house. It is not unknown for one to email the other to arrange to meet in the kitchen for a drink. Big houses contribute to our isolation. Everyone needs some of their own space, but today's big houses serve to keep family members apart because there is less need to be together.

The desire for larger, more luxurious and better located houses has been the main reason for the dramatic rise in house prices since the late 1990s. As more people set their hearts on bigger and better homes they bid up the price of the housing available, and to have what they want they must take out bigger mortgages. This means they commit a larger share of their future income to buying the house of their dreams. For the first time in our history we have a housing affordability crisis at a time of record high incomes and record low interest rates.

House & Garden magazine has captured the new mood: 'By purchasing high-price, high-profile furniture, people are not only treating themselves to the thrill of the big spend and a beautiful object, they're also creating an environment which makes them feel special'.[4] Redundant rooms must be filled with furnishings, appliances, carpets and curtains. They must be heated, cooled and cleaned. This adds to the time, money and energy needed for maintenance and requires extended shopping forays in order to fill the rooms up. For instance, sales of big screen televisions have been propelled by the prevalence of cavernous lounge rooms. Do larger houses on smaller blocks of land mean we can expect to see the ride-on lawnmower replaced by the ride-on vacuum cleaner?

A grander house must be fitted with luxurious furnishings: 'What was once considered extravagance is now considered the norm'.[5] The number, quality and complexity of home appliances have increased along with the rapidly expanding sales of luxury furnishings. Australians are no longer satisfied with standard appliances and are demanding high-quality professional ones. Instead of a $20 percolator we buy $500 espresso machines; instead of a standard gas or electric stove, kitchens are adorned with ovens featuring six cooking functions, turbo grills, touch controls, triple-glazed doors and the ability to defrost food before cooking it. Once confined to the houses of the rich, these are now marketed to average households, and many are paying $3000 or more for the pleasure. The professional-style Fisher & Paykel Quantum stainless steel double oven with cooker and hood retails for $6999. Some new homes are now marketed as having two kitchens—one an $80 000 stainless steel showcase for the latest European appliances never to be sullied by having food cooked in it and around the corner a cheaper one where the food is actually cooked (or the takeaway reheated).

Retailers of whitegoods now sell standard refrigerators for $700 to $800, more advanced models for $1200 to $2000, and luxury models such as the Maytag Side-by-Side Zigzag with stainless steel doors for $5399. Although refrigerators priced at $4000 or more sell well in certain markets, their primary purpose is to escalate the level of desire on the part of the ordinary customer. Instead of paying $800 for a fridge that would satisfy their needs perfectly well, customers pay $1600 or $2000 for one that has only marginally better performance. The higher price is interpreted as signifying higher quality and leaves the customer feeling they have a higher social status. Retailers can be quite explicit about the fact that the only difference between the high- and low-priced products is the perceptions associated with each brand.

Increasingly, the kitchen in the home is being duplicated by super-barbecues promoted as the 'kitchen outdoors'. A 1980s barbecue was typically assembled at home, with bricks, a hot plate and a storage area for wood. In the late 1990s a top-of-the-line model might have sold for $2000. Today Barbeques Galore sells the Turbo Cosmopolitan, described as 'Australia's most prestigious gourmet outdoor entertainment system', for $4990. Made of vitreous enamel, it boasts electronic multi-spark ignition in each of the six burners, deluxe cast-iron plates and a roasting hood with a 'dual glass window'. It can roast, smoke, bake and grill. But even this feature has been superseded: the Grand Turbo features an infra-red rotisserie rear burner and a price tag of $6990.

Although few of these highly sophisticated barbecues might be sold, their existence serves to drive up the level of desire. After admiring the Turbo Cosmopolitan or the Grand Turbo, customers are more likely to buy the Cordon Bleu for $1299—'the latest look in barbeques and one of our top sellers'—instead of paying $200 to $300 for a standard model. An advertisement for Rinnai's Monaco Outdoor Kitchen, retail price $2399, declares, 'I love the look on the neighbours' face when I roll out the Rinnai'. Australians today can spend more on a set of tongs for the barbecue than they spent on the barbecue itself in 1980.

There is something unsettling about a $7000 barbecue. The barbecue has traditionally served as the symbol of Australian egalitarianism. It represented the place where Australians could gather for the simple purpose of cultivating and enjoying their relationships with family members and friends. Unpretentious, convivial, reflective, in a quiet way the barbecue was where Australians celebrated their culture. All that is destroyed when the barbecue becomes an opportunity to outdo the neighbours and other family members, where the objective is not so much to share a meal cooked before the gaze of those we are close to but instead to engage in an ostentatious display of worldly success. Yet these super-barbecues are 'flying out the doors' of the retailers.

Inside the home, sales of big screen televisions and home theatres have boomed in recent years. In 1998 the price of top-of-the-range television sets was between $1500 and $2000; now they cost over $6000. Many consumers have stepped up to plasma-screen televisions, at a cost of $9000 or more. It is not unusual for customers to enter a shop with a budget of $4500 and end up spending twice as much. A 37-inch Sharp LCD TV retails at $8999, while the Yamaha DPX-1—'The World's best home cinema projector'—is priced at $16 995. Instead of spending a few hundred dollars or perhaps a thousand on a new television, the level of desire has escalated and people think they must spend several thousand dollars to get what they need.

> Keith Pike, a Sydney architect who specialises in new homes, sees the TV being included in every room except the living room. He says, 'The TV has come out of the living room because that's for entertainment, and instead goes into the purpose-built media room'.[6]

Our relentless acquisition of 'stuff' is outgrowing the capacity of our ever-growing houses. This has given rise to a booming self-storage industry. A few years ago the self-storage industry in Australia was in its infancy compared with the United States, but it has been growing at 10 per cent a year compared with the economy's overall growth rate of between 3 and 4 per cent. The Self-Storage Association of Australasia reports that there are more than 1000 self-storage centres in Australia and that 75 per cent of the customers are residential rather than commercial. Most of the space is hired to store household items such as furniture, whitegoods, clothes and personal effects.

Ourselves

In the 1990s sunglasses became a symbol of identity, replacing the cigarette as the statement of cool. Two hundred dollars for a pair is now regarded as cheap. A pair of Oakley X Metal XX 'eyewear' retails for $699.95, or more if you opt for titanium dioxide plating or a 24-carat gold finish. They are 'the only 3-D sculptured, hypoallergenic, all-metal frames on earth'. Not everyone can afford $700, but many people are willing to fork out $449 for a pair of Oakley X Metal Juliets (an extra $100 for the case) or $336 for Gucci rimless 1494s. It is not unusual for young men and women with weekly incomes of $420 to spend $450 on a pair of sunglasses and to own two or three pairs. Those who can't really afford the expense will justify it with statements such as 'I couldn't find anything else to suit me' or 'They were expensive but they will last a lot longer'. More self-aware consumers might be inclined to say, 'I was sucked in by the image, but what the hell'.

There is a trend for manufacturers of luxury goods to make entry-level products in an effort to attract consumers other than the very rich. Gucci and Armani attach their name to sunglasses that are bought by people who cannot afford to buy clothes or accessories with such a prestigious label. This is sometimes referred to as the 'democratisation of luxury': the people who buy the entry-level products feel they can emulate the image of the very rich. Car makers such as Mercedes and BMW are manufacturing models that middle-income households can afford. For example, the Mercedes C180 Classic retails for a mere $51 800 and the A-class for only $35 000. At the other end of the spectrum, the Mercedes Maybach 62 costs more than $650 000 and the brochure for it $400. The car has been developed for a very small segment of the market. 'They are people like movie stars, they are entrepreneurs, they are industry giants,' says the president of Mercedes-Benz in the United States. The company expects to sell no more than 1000 Maybachs a year; in fact, low sales are the goal:

In the jargon of automobile marketing, the Maybach is a 'halo' car, adding an aura of exclusivity to some of the less expensive cars sold by its parent company, DaimlerChrysler. Analysts point out that even the once revered Mercedes name has been diluted somewhat. With 200 000 Mercedes on the road in the US, it's just not as special as it used to be.

Rings for the right hand are an emerging fashion statement, one promoted by diamond miner De Beers, which saw its market limited by the fact that women typically acquire expensive rings only when men buy them for them. Exploiting the politics of feminism, the advertising campaign set out to create the belief that a right-hand ring symbolises freedom for women. In fact, the independence De Beers touted is more a manifestation of self-centred isolation: 'Your left hand says we, your right hand says me' runs one of the ads. One starry-eyed commentator wrote that the ads 'mark the creation of the Me-Ring, as brilliant and expensive as an engagement ring, only symbolising independence, not alliance. It is a token of love from you to yourself'.[7] It would be hard to find a better definition of narcissism. The advertising campaign has been a huge success in the United States, where upmarket jewellers are selling US$5000 rings 'faster than we can get them'. In Australia, well-heeled women are buying rocks for their 'bling fingers'.

The right-hand ring is an illustration of how attuned the market is to social movements that open people up to new consumption possibilities. Through all its phases, feminism has been a marketing bonanza. The growth in the number of single-parent families as a result of higher divorce rates has been carefully analysed in order to understand how consumption decisions are made when there is no adult partner to consult. Every anti-establishment cultural innovation, from rap music to rock climbing, is colonised and exploited by the marketers. Rebellion has become one of the emotions targeted by marketers, who unashamedly turn attempts to escape the fetters of convention into their exact opposite. Diesel jeans are marketed as the uniform of the antiglobalisation movement. Corporate advertisers use graffiti as a marketing technique. Those who want to cultivate spirituality can do so on a Louis Vuitton yoga mat, which comes with its own carry bag, for $2700. Perhaps the most poignant example is the commercial appropriation of Che Guevara's image: the quintessential emblem of youthful rebellion has been transformed into a cute symbol of postmodern individuality.

Our pets

Our pets are increasingly becoming a reflection of our lifestyle choices, the image we want to project to the world. This has always been true to a degree—'I am a cat person', for example—but nowadays we are far more discriminating about the message our choice of pet sends about the type of person we imagine we are. Our spending on pets is a means of investing in our self-image, a fact that is far more apparent to the makers and marketers of products for pets than it is to pet owners. Affluenza has infected this aspect of our lives too.

Sixty-four per cent of Australian households own one or more pets. We share our homes with an estimated 3.6 million dogs, 2.3 million cats, 7.5 million birds and 13.2 million fish.[8] But growth in the number of pets accounts for only a small proportion of the growth in expenditure on pet food and pet-related products, which has been stimulated mainly by increased purchases of premium pet foods. A recent analysis of the pet food industry found, 'The majority of pet carers are female, married with children, living in the suburbs and mostly employed, indicating that pet owners are extremely busy juggling their personal and professional lifestyles, and obliged to feed their pets premium food'. The report does not expand on why busy female pet owners would feel 'obliged' to buy premium pet food, but it seems that guilt associated with the lack of time and attention paid to pets is a factor—in the same way that parents often try to compensate for spending too much time away from their children by buying them things.

Australians spent more than $1.5 billion on pet food and pet care products in 2003, most of it on food for dogs and cats. This figure does not include buying the pets or the cost of services such as veterinary care, boarding kennels, pet grooming and tooth-cleaning services. Total expenditure on pets is estimated to have been well over $2.3 billion in 2003, an amount that might be compared with the $2 billion Australia spends on overseas aid each year.[9] While most Australian consumers feel unable to meet all their own needs, spending on pet food and pet care products is huge and growing, with more and more emphasis on luxury products.

Pet food manufacturers work hard to develop 'super pre-mium' pet foods with the intention of encouraging consumers to stop buying cheaper products or, at a minimum, start buying mid-priced products. The Australian cat food industry, faced with a decline in the number of cats, might phase out low-priced cat food altogether in order to ensure that the reduced volume of food sales can still deliver increases in revenue:

> Increasing volume and value sales of premium cat food and cat treats indicate that cat owners value their feline companions

more than ever, and are constantly seeking ways of rewarding their cats for the joy and companionship they give. Economy products are likely to be slowly phased out, and mid-priced products will stagnate. It is also very likely that the majority of new products introduced will be in the premium price segment.

The same applies to dog food, where growth in disposable incomes and effective advertising—rather than an increase in the number of dogs—are the key to increasing expenditure on dog food.

Table 1 provides an indication of the range of luxury pet products now available. Dog treats can cost over $100 a kilogram. Pet jewellery priced at over $800 can be ordered online. Among the other products available are fish food that is engineered to sink more slowly than usual, so fish that prefer to eat at different depths can be catered for; energy treats for turtles; and antiflatulence tablets for dogs.

The 'needs' yet to be satisfied in the pet product industry may be as limitless as humans' 'needs'. A report on the industry observes, 'Convenient grooming wipes also promise to reduce time spent washing, brushing and combing pets, whilst the launch of products such as Rinaldo Franco's sleeping bags for ferrets in Italy offers unprecedented levels of comfort for spoiled pets'.

The belief that humans can establish closer emotional bonds with their pets through buying expensive pet foods and toys reflects the 'humanisation' of pets. Dogs and cats are increasingly cared for according to human patterns and human aesthetics. They are regarded as family members and are often considered equivalent to, or substitutes for, children in terms of the level of attention they receive from their owners. The development of cosmetics for pets illustrates the trend, with new products such as bath wipes, scented shampoos and nail polish for dogs coming onto the market.

Table 1: Some luxury pet products

Product	Manufacturer's description	Price
Oral care fish treats from Inobys	. . . safe and effective, easy to use treat that freshens your cat's breath while helping to reduce plaque and tartar	$8.95 for 100 g
Cheddar cheese snacks	Cheese snacks for pets	$3.45 for 50 g
Bacon Bitz	Kick off the day the Bacon Bitz way, with this delicious new treat from Schmackos! . . . Served whole or torn into pieces, Bacon Bitz are delicious meaty treats that have been air dried to really seal in the flavour to send your dog wacko!	$3.95 for 100 g
K-9 Float Coat	Ruff Wear believes four-legged companions deserve the same level of safety and protection afforded by life jackets for humans. The K-9 Float Coat is high-performance flotation for canine water safety	$122.00

continued

Table 1 *continued*

Product	Manufacturer's description	Price
Bow Wow Dog Treats pigs' ears	Dried pigs' ears	$2.15 for 20 g
Aristopet pet cologne	Fifi for girls: Sweet fresh fragrance like Tea Rose Perfume Fido for Boys: A little like Brut Aftershave for men	$7.20 for 125 ml
Puppy Luv	Nine-carat gold heart with diamond designer name tag	$875.00
Hero dog fragrance	A distinctly masculine fragrance for your dog or cat with a long-lasting pleasant aroma. Great finishing touch to your grooming or for a spruce up between baths	$12.95 for 500 ml
Iams Light Dry Food	A premium food designed for overweight adult cats or cats that are less active and require less energy. It has reduced fat and calories for weight loss or maintenance	$9.50 for 650 g

Much of the impulse to anthropomorphise pets finds its origins in the desire to demonstrate love for them, a desire that in more affluent markets, such as those of America and Australia, increasingly finds expression in an urge to 'spoil' pets. In the process, the owners project their desires onto their pets, and these desires must then be fulfilled. The owner reaps a double reward—a feeling of wellbeing from having done something for the animal and the gratification that comes from any demonstration of affection by the pet. Yet there is no evidence that pets appreciate a $50 toy more than a $5 toy. Perhaps their inability to tell their owners to stop will ensure that growth in such expenditure will accelerate as incomes continue to grow and birth rates decline. The down-shifting dog is a long way off.

Our children

Parents are tending to project their search for identity onto their children. In some wealthier areas babies now wear designer clothes, so that the babies themselves have become a fashion accessory. The Posh Baby brand markets its products 'for the hip baby in the crib—groovy blankets, burp cloths and change mats in the funkiest fabrics'. One parent reported how thrilled she was at the special service she received in shops because of her 'funky' toddler, Ponie, who was wearing 'a pink cashmere cardigan, striped Genko T-shirt and miniature Vans runners from Japan'.[10] She added, 'She is wearing the worst shoes for her outfit, but I let her go.' Ponie was 2½ years old at the time.

Babies are indifferent to the design features of the blankets they vomit on, and 2-year-olds do not appreciate the symbolism of an 'Alice Temperly-look broderie anglaise dress with ribbon tie'.

Babies and toddlers are dressed in brand-named clothes solely for the benefit of the parents, who, through their children, communicate to the world the type of person they want to be seen to be. This might be harmless fun, but it is more likely that parents are imposing their own vanities on their children, telling themselves they are using designer brands to give their children an 'individual' identity but in reality passing on their own insecurities. Individualism imposed from above is, of course, a contradiction.

Children dressed in thousand-dollar outfits are less likely to play football in the park—although they might end up being sent to a gym. With governments pressuring school canteens to limit junk food, including soft drinks, parents and citizens groups are promoting brand-named bottled water, relegating the bubbler to curio status and creating a mound of plastic bottles that take millennia to degrade.

The values of the market have penetrated the relationships between parents and their children. Spurred on by the calculations of economic research agencies, modern parents are acutely aware of how much their children are 'costing them'. Sometimes the children are blamed for causing financial pain. When they read that the cost of raising a child is $300 000, or some equally scary sum, some parents feel that having children is a burden and that, at a minimum, they deserve tax relief to compensate for their reproductive choice.

In the 2004 budget the Federal Government announced it would pay a $3000 lump sum to women when they have a baby (rising to $4000 in 2006 and $5000 in 2008). This led some women to reschedule their caesareans so that they would qualify for the payment. (Incidentally, some of those caesareans had been planned for cosmetic rather than medical reasons—a practice described as 'too posh to push'.) The Treasurer said that the best way to support low-income earners is to help with their family responsibilities (although the payment is not means tested) and that the new Maternity Allowance recognises the financial burden of having a child and would help parents with their childcare bills. 'This is aimed squarely at the family which is struggling with juggling work and family,' he said.[11] The Government subsequently announced an additional family bonus of $600 per child. When that payment was made to families in July 2004, newspapers across the country carried commentary such as the following:

> Victorians spent more on pokies in the week that the $600 family bonus was issued than in any other week of the year, adding fuel to claims that some of the money was lost on gambling.[12]
>
> The nation has gone on a spending spree since the Federal Government's $600-a-child payment landed in parents' bank accounts last week, although it appears that not all of it is being spent on children.
>
> People are also using the largesse to splurge on mobile phones or even big-ticket items like television sets. Some are spending up big at pubs or clubs, with reports that the windfall has caused particular chaos in the Northern Territory.[13]

Such commentary illustrates the contrast between the image of the struggling family constructed by Australia's political leaders and the real circumstances of most Australians.

Chapter 3
Spreading the virus

If it makes you happy it's a bargain.
It's not your fault you love everything, you're just a
positive person. In fact, we have so many pro-
purchase customers at WBJ we've created Handsfree
Shopping . . . You can now shop, shop and shop
without carrying a single bag.
——advertisement for Westfield Bondi Junction
shopping centre

Manufacturing desire

The working lives of Australia's best-paid psychologists are not devoted to treating the distress of people with psychological problems: they are devoted to developing ways of increasing consumers' insecurity, vulnerability and obsessiveness. They work in marketing. Neoliberal economists insist that advertising is valuable because it provides information for consumers, but people working in the industry readily concede that it is far more effective to make people feel inadequate than it is to inform them about the useful features of a product. Although we can all recognise the value of a catchy jingle or a clever slogan, few of us are aware of just how far—and sometimes how low—advertisers are willing to go to increase sales.

Advertising is but one of the functions of the marketing industry, and it has in fact been declining in importance. In the past two to three decades consumers have become increasingly resistant to overt attempts to persuade them to buy things. Young people who have grown up in age of media saturation are particularly resistant to being advertised at; they don't want to be seen to be the dupes of anyone, although they can still be persuaded to pay hundreds of dollars for trainers that the retailers admit are identical to ones that are a quarter of the price. Marketers have had to find new ways of making their messages credible and new ways of duping those savvier kids.

Sometimes advertisers try to make us laugh or make us think, but mostly they make us feel deprived, inadequate or anxious. It is axiomatic that they make us feel bad in a way that can be cured by possession of the product they advertise. Some of the strategies they use are quite obvious: 'Don't like your body? Buy this weight loss plan.' 'Going bald? Get this treatment.' But strategies can be far subtler and far more effective. Lifestyle programs reinforce the message of advertising by making us feel discontented about the size of our house or the quality of our appliances. Ads by cosmetic companies encourage us to believe that only the young in appearance can have happy relationships and be successful at work—although with the advent of Botox, which really does get rid of wrinkles, makers of anti-wrinkle creams have begun to point out how much character older faces have. Wrinkles now need to be 'softened' rather than removed.

Marketing has become a dominant feature of modern culture. The messages are everywhere we look—sporting events, building walls, petrol pumps, cultural events, street pavements, the sides of vans and buses, and school canteens, not to mention in all forms of media and in shopping centres themselves. It is estimated that the average American receives 9000 advertising messages a day, and Australians are not far behind. Marketing goes much further than delivering a plethora of messages to assault our eyes and ears: it imbues almost everything and is impossible to escape. Indeed, Western culture can be described as a marketing culture and, as we will see, the advent of the marketing society is strongly correlated with the rise in depression, anxiety, obesity and a range of other disorders. The marketing culture is indispensable to the daily spread of affluenza.

In her book *No Logo*, Naomi Klein describes the process whereby producers of consumer goods progressively offload all aspects of the actual manufacturing process by contracting out, especially to factories in the Third World. They concentrate their efforts on creating and sustaining the intangible features of consumer products that give them most of their value, that is, the brand. Marketing has become the foundation on which large corporations are now built. In the 1990s marketing transformed the mundane and functional whitegoods of down-market Korean manufacturer Lucky Goldstar into the hip lifestyle accessories made by LG. Without marketing, Nike shoes would be indistinguishable from a dozen other makes. As Coles Myer, one of Australia's largest retailers, admitted to an official inquiry:

> ... non-branded footwear often incorporates the same or similar methods of construction, technology and components/materials. Moreover, it is often sourced from the same factory as branded footwear. The commercial reality is that without the brand the consumer perceives no value that warrants a premium price.[1]

After an independent test of running shoes costing from $30 to $230, one tester stated, 'We find that in every single test we do here, price is no guide to quality or performance'.[2] It is marketing that transforms generic goods into brands and thereby transfers much of the benefit of globalisation from factory workers in the Third World to shareholders of corporations headquartered in New York, Tokyo or Sydney.

Large corporations rely on marketing to solve two problems. First, it is used to ensure that consumers never shop primarily on price. As the former head of a major Australian corporation said, 'Orderly marketing is a built-in feature of how we do business in Australia. We have to keep our margins up. The Australian marketplace is too small to cut each other's throats. If we get into a price war with [a competitor], the only winner is the customer'.[3] Second, marketers seek to create 'brand loyalty', whereby individual consumers develop an emotional relationship with a brand, a relationship based on trust or even—if we are to believe Kevin Roberts, head of Saatchi and Saatchi, one of the world's largest advertising companies—a relationship based on love. Asked to define love, Roberts replied:

> Beyond price, value, benefits, attributes, performance, distribution. You have to stay loyal to the idea of something because . . . because nothing. Because that's how you feel. Three months ago, I was in Seattle talking to 3000 professors and afterwards I walked past an Adidas concept store. I love Adidas. I didn't need anything, didn't want anything. $US880 later I walked out of that store.[4]

Most economists construct worlds in which rational consumers make decisions based on good information about the merits of the products they buy; marketers assume the opposite. The unspoken role of marketing is to keep consumers in the richest societies in human history feeling deprived. To be successful in the long term, advertising must sell not only products but also a very particular kind of world view—one where happiness can be bought, where problems can be solved by a product, and where having more things is the measure of success.

'More choice is good' is the mantra of the politicians and economists who have created the world in the neoliberal image. Deification of consumer choice has meant steadily growing numbers of brands and varieties of yoghurt, washing powder, cars and runners. There are 49 types of olive oil on sale at the local supermarket, and anyone entering a sports shoe shop is bamboozled by an extraordinary display of footwear apparently designed to meet every need.

After the wave of privatisations in the 1980s and 1990s, instead of a single reliable publicly-owned phone or electricity company, we are forced to choose and to wrestle with a suspicion that we are probably being ripped off. If we had the time to carry out systematic market research we could probably save ourselves a few dollars, but we would have to repeat the process every few months to keep up with the market. Faced with this proliferation of choice, most consumers just feel confused. If anyone actually behaved in this 'rational' way we would think they needed to get a life.

The explosion of choice serves a crucial function: it spreads affluenza. It does this by creating desires, intensifying the feeling of deprivation, and hastening obsolescence. People suffering from affluenza do not know what they want, yet want everything. More choice helps create new desires by highlighting the range of products consumers could have. Rather than being content with a twin-blade razor, shoppers are now tempted by razors with three and even four blades. The five-blade razor is yet to reach the market, but when it does men will be faced with another choice, and it is impossible to imagine that this extra choice will add to their sense of wellbeing. While some choice is beneficial, too much can actually cause a decline in wellbeing. In an experiment in which subjects had to pick a chocolate from a selection of 30, the sense of regret and uncertainty about whether they had chosen the 'most delicious' chocolate was greater than that experienced by a group who chose from a selection of only six different types of chocolate.[5]

The psychology of marketing

In one of history's best-known experiments Russian physiologist Ivan Pavlov conditioned dogs by sounding a bell while presenting them with food. After the procedure had been repeated several times the dogs would begin to salivate as soon as they heard the bell. Advertisers are well aware of the value of association: 'If you think what Pavlov did, he actually took a neutral object and, by associating it with a meaningful object, made it a symbol of something else; he imbued it with imagery, he gave it added value, and isn't that what we try and do in modern advertising?'[6]

One of the most powerful tools in the advertisers' armoury is the capacity to link margarine, soft drinks, jeans and cars with the kinds of emotions most people like to feel. Researchers have discovered that the brand associations we learn become 'hard-wired' into our minds. In a disturbing experiment by neuroscientists, the subjects' brains were scanned using magnetic resonance imaging while they drank Coca-Cola and Pepsi.[7] When the subjects drank unbranded brown carbonated sugar waters—which they could not distinguish from one another by their taste alone—only the taste-sensing part of the brain, the ventromedial pre-frontal cortex, was activated. But other parts of the brain became active when the subjects could see the Coke brand and believed they were drinking Coke. The imaging showed the hippocampus, the dorsolateral pre-frontal cortex and the midbrain, parts of the brain associated with memory and responses to visual cues, lighting up as well. It was observed that this reaction occurred with Coke but not with Pepsi, and only when Coke was identified as Coke. It did not occur when the subjects were unaware that they were drinking Coke.

Decades of marketing by Coca-Cola have conditioned the human brain to experience pleasure from drinking Coke as a result of the cultural messages associated with the product, quite independently of the actual sensory experience. (If you doubt the power of the cultural meaning associated with Coke, try taking a bottle of generic cola to a party and note how others judge you. Pour the generic cola into a Coke bottle and you will receive social approval and save money.) The ability of Coke, but not Pepsi, to activate these other areas of the brain explains why Coke is preferred by more people, even though it is distinguishable only by the brand.

Coca-Cola has found the Holy Grail of marketing: it has managed to embed in our culture such a powerful set of associations and meanings for its product that it can activate parts of the brain its competitors cannot reach. We have not so much been brainwashed into drinking Coca-Cola: we have had our brains rewired to want it.

Advertisers persistently link margarine with images of families, healthy children and 'quality time'. Breakfasts are made, kids jump on parents' beds, and the sun streams through the windows. Most parents know that when children make breakfast in bed for them the result will probably be burnt toast, a mess in the kitchen and tea spilt over the doona, yet advertisers know the approach works because it is the emotion, not the margarine, that is being sold.

No one would admit to believing that buying a certain brand of margarine will secure a happy family life. They know that all margarine consists of vegetable oil, salt and food colouring and is sold in plastic tubs of similar size and shape. Manufacturers have difficulty differentiating their products, so instead they create a distinct image associated with the product. Some margarines are marketed to young families and some to young singles in a hurry. The substances are the same, but the emotions attached to them are carefully chosen—joyous families together, nostalgia for times spent with grandpa, loving mothers nurturing their children, no-fuss living for young singles. All these things can be found in a tub of vegetable fat.

Deconstructing car advertisements is almost too easy. Ads for cars rarely show more than one car on the road at a time, unless the vehicle in question is leaving others in its wake. In defiance of the reality of being stuck in a traffic jam, cars are often sold as symbols of freedom—the freedom to go wherever you want, whenever you want and usually, on the ads at least, as fast as you want. One of the least subtle car advertisements screened in Australia depicted a young man getting into his big black Jeep Cherokee to drive to work. On the way, his car morphs into a black stallion, which he rides across the wild plains. Arriving at work, the stallion turns back into a car and Stallion Man miraculously finds a parking space right in front of his office. As he steps from the car an attractive woman approaches to brush from his jacket the dust that had accumulated while he was riding his steed to work.

The message is clear to the most inattentive of viewers: even a nine-to-five wage slave can live out cowboy fantasies and appeal to attractive women if he buys a large, inefficient and expensive car to crawl through peak hour traffic each day. The role of persuasion and emotion in advertising was described in the following way:

> One of the striking tendencies of human beings is to act, judge, believe or vote on strictly instinctive, emotional grounds, and then, after the act is committed, to try to justify or defend it by intellectual or logical reasons . . . Men buy automobiles in the same way. I buy my car because my neighbour has one, because it will gratify my vanity or satisfy my pride. Then, having bought the car, I look about for logical justifications which I can give for my conduct.[8]

Advertisers have become adept at playing to the heart while providing excuses for the head. For example, despite the overwhelming evidence that large 4WDs are more dangerous for both their occupants and other road users, advertisers succeed in playing to car buyers' need for personal safety while at the same time extolling practical benefits such as luggage capacity, visibility for the driver, and the ability to take the family away on camping trips. (When asked whether he ever took his 4WD off-road, one owner said, 'Yes, of course. I park it in the drive every night'.)

US market research into people who buy large 4WDs shows that they tend to be 'insecure and vain':

> They are frequently nervous about their marriages and uncomfortable about parenthood. They often lack confidence in their driving skills. Above all, they are apt to be self-centered and self-absorbed, with little interest in their neighbors and communities. They are more restless, more sybaritic, and less social than most Americans are. They tend to like fine restaurants a lot more than off-road driving, seldom go to church and have limited interest in doing volunteer work to help others.[9]

The manufacturers of large 4WDs use marketing messages to hide the reality of poor safety, handling and fuel economy behind a veneer of security, confidence and quality family time. These are the things the psychologists know potential buyers want; the advertisers know they must sell beliefs rather than behemoths.

In the face of all this, the marketing culture nevertheless carries the seeds of its own negation because at some level the modern consumer is aware that the sense of identity derived from consumption activity is completely lacking in authenticity. To counter this, some marketers set out to persuade consumers that owning particular products is a sign of rebellion against social orthodoxies—hoping the consumers will not realise they are being asked to believe that the dull conformity of consumer society can be transcended through another act of consumption. The clothing brand known as FCUK is an example. The marketing experts developed a strategy of appealing to young people by deliberately offending staider members of the community. Buying and wearing the brand would mean giving the finger to conventional society, as if uttering a profanity in public is an assertion of independence. This is the sort of tame 'rebellion' modern consumerism thrives on.

Creating an association between something desirable and a particular product might sound easy, but marketing psychologists are always searching for more sophisticated ways of doing so. One recent approach relies on the creation of fake memories of childhood. We are helped to invent an association between our childhood selves and the product in question and then, so as to relive our carefree childhood years, we are encouraged to consume the product all over again. Testing whether it is possible for marketers to create childhood 'memories', a team of psychologists in the United States found that experimental subjects who were shown advertisements suggesting they had shaken hands with Mickey Mouse as children were more likely than a control group to believe that they had actually done so.[10]

To ensure that the advertisements were not acting simply as a prompt that helped people recall legitimate memories, a number of other experiments were conducted. Each had surprising results. In one, subjects were exposed to an advertisement that showed them shaking hands with an impossible character, such as Bugs Bunny at a Disney resort. (Bugs Bunny is owned by Warner Brothers, so the encounter could not occur.) Even so, the subjects exposed to the ads were more likely than the controls to 'remember' such an encounter.

Advertisers rely on psychologists to learn more about our subconscious desires, our weaknesses and our insecurities than we ourselves know. They rely too on our capacity for self-deception, our memories (even if they have to be created) and our yearning for social acceptance. Marketing is the process through which our desire for more is perpetuated; it is the vector that carries the affluenza virus. Its function is twofold. It persuades us to buy specific products and it delivers the subliminal message that happiness can be had from acquiring things. Marketing sells materialism using the ultimate form of Pavlovian association—buying stuff equals happiness.

In this way, our marketing culture has done something profound right under our noses: it has redefined happiness itself. In place of the time-honoured belief that a happy life is one of fulfilment acquired through developing our capacities, cultivating personal relationships and adhering to a moral code, people today have been persuaded that a happy life is one in which we maximise the number of episodes of emotional and physical pleasure, however fleeting they might be.

Tinys, tweens and teens

> Advertisements to children must not state or imply that a Product makes Children who own or enjoy it superior to their peers.
>
> ——Australian Association of National Advertisers,
> Code for Advertising to Children

Childhood has become a 'marketing free-fire zone', and the lounge room is the kindergarten of consumerism. We all know about the pressure on children to consume. What is less understood is how the thick fog of commercial messages in which children now grow up conditions their understanding of the world and themselves. The impact of advertising on young people has been a topic of debate since the 1970s, but the advertising industry's most recent assault on children has resulted in both renewed interest on the part of researchers and renewed opposition from parents' groups. As with most things related to the advertising industry, the United States is about five years ahead of the rest of the affluent world. A look at current trends in that country provides a taste of things to come in Australia.

Whereas marketers once pitched their advertisements for children's breakfast cereal at mothers—on the basis that parents decide what their children should consume—modern marketers often aim their advertising at children in the belief that the children will then play on their parents' weaknesses and cajole them into buying the product in question. This is more than a strategy for selling children's products: it is also designed to sell adult goods—including cars, home appliances and holidays. Juliet Schor, one of the most vocal critics of the US advertising industry's increasing focus on children, argues that marketers see children not just as a lucrative demographic but also as the weakest link in the defences families build up to protect themselves against marketing.[11]

This targeting of children in order to sell adult products has recently been tried in Australia. The well-known disinfectant Dettol is now marketed explicitly to children by promoting a fear of 'germs', germs that only Dettol can protect them from. One of the first of these advertisements showed a child making a documentary in which plastic spiders and caterpillars were used to depict germs on toilet seats and other household surfaces. Another child carrying a hose with a large Dettol sign attached to the nozzle then arrives to clean away the germs. A subsequent advertisement showed close-ups of children playing in the 'dirty' backyard, touching, among other things, a tennis ball that had been in a dog's mouth. A naive viewer might think this is an appeal to anxious parents, but the object is actually to create anxious children. Fear is instilled in the children, and they are then provided with the argument they need to convince their parents to buy a particular product. After all, most parents will take steps to allay their children's fears, even if those fears are exaggerated.

Research in the United States shows that this is just the beginning. The value of purchases made by 4- to 12-year-olds increased from US$6.1 billion in 1989 to $30 billion in 2002[12] but—more importantly for the marketers—children directly influence how $330 billion of their parents' incomes will be spent. The role of marketing to children is widely acknowledged in the advertising industry: 'Kids are wielding influence like we've never seen in the marketplace before. It's not just a 55 cent candy bar or a box of cereal anymore. Very young consumers affect purchases of $10 000, $20 000, $30 000 products'.[13] Indeed, the owner of a string of car dealerships in the United States has said:

> The kids decide what's cool, and parents don't want to seem out of touch, so they listen. Sometimes, the child literally is our customer. I have watched the child pick out the car. And I have seen people go from a Taurus to an Explorer in the blink of an eye because the kid didn't want to be seen in a station wagon.[14]

One industry estimate has it that 67 per cent of parents' car purchases are influenced by children.[15] When this was realised some years ago, ads for products usually chosen by adults began to be targeted at children. A recent television advertisement for the high-sugar breakfast cereal Coco Pops featured Monica Trapaga, a much-loved presenter from the ABC's children's program *Play*

School, informing young viewers that Coco Pops contain no artificial colours and are a good source of calcium, iron, and vitamins B1 and B2. Despite the advertisers' code of ethics stipulating that advertisements for food and beverages 'must not contain any misleading or incorrect information about the nutritional value' of a product,[16] the advertisers failed to mention the sugar content. The advertisement relies on a former star of *Play School* to portray Coco Pops as a nutritious food, and the company's website says that Coco, the monkey mascot, 'loves Coco Pops not only because of its delicious chocolatey taste, but also because it contains essential vitamins and minerals . . .'[17] The purpose of these advertisements is to equip children with the argument they need to overcome any parental concern about feeding their children a breakfast cereal that contains more than 36 per cent sugar.[18]

FIGURE 2: Inverting the pyramid—healthy eating versus food advertising to children

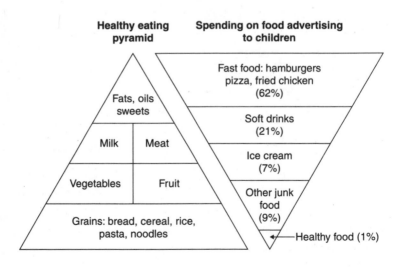

The advertisers promote eating habits that directly contradict the advice of nutritionists, a fact illustrated by Figure 2.[19] Ninety-nine per cent of food advertisements directed at children are for junk food—hamburgers, pizza, fried chicken, soft drinks, ice cream and chocolate confectionery.[20] The healthy eating programs sponsored by government struggle in vain to counteract the effects of slick marketing and appealing to the weaknesses of children and their parents. Yet, because this is the market speaking, our political leaders are reluctant to put a stop to it.

Busy parents are not the only victims of marketing to children: the children themselves are the target of the psychologists employed by the advertising companies. The children's vulnerability is important to the marketers:

> Advertising at its best is making people feel that, without their product, you're a loser. Kids are very sensitive to that. If you tell them to buy something, they are resistant. But if you tell them they'll be a dork if they don't, you've got their attention. You open up emotional vulnerabilities, and it's easy to do with kids because they're the most vulnerable.[21]

The marketers consider that shaping the behaviour and world view of children is profitable not just in the short term. In an unconscious reprise of the old Jesuit saying 'Give me a child until he is seven, and I will give you the man', the president of toy retailer Kids-R-Us once said, 'If you own this child at an early age, you can own this child for years to come. Companies are saying "Hey, I want to own the kid younger and younger" '.[22]

The idea of reaching and 'owning' children at younger and younger ages has a long history in the tobacco industry. Even in the

1970s the link between the psychological vulnerability of children and a good advertising campaign was well understood, as the following comments from a tobacco marketing executive reveal:

> . . . a new brand aimed at the young smoker must somehow become the 'in' brand and its promotion should emphasise togetherness, belonging and group acceptance, while at the same time emphasising individuality and 'doing one's own thing'. The teens and early twenties are periods of intense psychological stress, restlessness and boredom. Many socially awkward situations are encountered. The minute or two required to stop and light a cigarette, ask for a light, find an ash tray, and the like provide something to do during periods of awkwardness and boredom . . .

The company was quite unapologetic about exploiting the vulnerabilities of teenagers in order to sell its product, which even then was known to be harmful:

> The fragile, developing self-image of the young person needs all of the support and enhancement it can get . . . a careful study of the current youth jargon, together with a review of currently used high school American history books and like sources for valued things might be a good start at finding a good brand name and image theme.[23]

Little has changed, although attention has now moved to pre-schoolers—known as 'tinys' in the world of marketing. Marketers target tinys because they know that 3-year-olds have considerable pester power, especially with parents who find it difficult to set clear rules. We now know that children as young as six months begin to form images of corporate logos. A recent British study found that for one in four children the first recognisable word they utter is a brand name.[24] A professor of marketing at the prestigious Texas A&M University claims that the invasion of the world of toddlers by marketing is no cause for alarm:

> The positive effect I see is that they are able to function in the marketplace at an earlier age. And in a full-blown developed, industrialized society, that's where we satisfy most of our needs—in the marketplace.[25]

Such a view makes one ask why reputable universities offer courses in marketing.

Some psychologists are becoming alarmed at the adverse impact of new strategies for advertising to children. Nagging is not just an irritation to be laughed off: it is being used to transform the relationship between parent and child. In particular, concern is being expressed about the way advertising depicts parents as obstacles for children to get around rather than as figures of authority whose opinions should be respected. In a well-known study, Cheryl Idell spelt out the role of the 'nag factor' in parental purchasing decisions.[26] She found that the majority of today's parents are influenced by their children's repeated requests—the usual number of requests is eight—for products. Half the 12- to 13-year-olds she surveyed said they were usually successful in convincing their parents to buy an advertised product they wanted, even if their parents didn't want them to have it.[27]

Perhaps it is the very effectiveness of the nagging strategy that has induced Australia's big advertisers to deny that this is what they do. Their Code for Advertising to Children declares that ads aimed at children 'must not undermine the authority, responsibility or judgement of parents or carers'. In fact, one of the best ways to find out which techniques work best is to look at the methods that are 'banned' by the Code. It is as though the advertisers salve their guilty consciences by formally proscribing the methods they use most often. If these voluntary codes were to become enforceable by law, almost all advertisements in Australia would be illegal.

In addition, advertisements sometimes encourage children to use emotional blackmail to wear down their parents. A shameless 1990s television advertisement for a financial institution showed a child asking her father for a new bike for Christmas. When the father reluctantly told the child he could not afford a new bike, the child replied that if he were to go to the financial institution in question he could get a special low-interest loan to cover the cost of Christmas presents. Use of strategies such as this is widespread. Two practising psychologists describe the difficulty in the following terms:

> In one of our practices . . . parents have approached the thera-
> pist in turmoil over how to respond to [such advertising]. They
> feel guilty about purchasing items, such as junk food or violent
> video games, which they believe are bad for their kids. On the
> other hand, they worry that by constantly saying 'no' they will
> increase their child's depression or worsen an already strained
> parent–child relationship.[28]

As well as these attempts to disrupt the nature of the parent–child relationship, there is growing concern that advertising itself has adverse effects on the wellbeing of children. Advertisers are more aware than anyone of many children's need to see themselves as 'cool'. The ability to demonstrate coolness through spending decisions is an important message that advertisers try to impart. But, to create a desire for a cool new product, the marketer must first engender discontent among the children who do not have the latest toy, sports shoe or breakfast cereal. Then they must convince the children that their lives will be better if they consume more. The result of this process is a generation of children who are fatter, more materialistic and more beset by behavioural problems than any generation that has preceded them.

Is it any wonder that children have short attention spans and many are diagnosed with attention deficit hyperactivity disorder? The purpose of advertising is to sell them something and then persuade them to move on to the next thing as soon as possible. Advertising to children infects the next generation with affluenza— and with a more virulent strain. It might succeed in creating lifetime brand loyalty, but it is also causing children to define their goals in material terms and eroding the bonds that unite parents and their children. When we consider the amount of time children spend watching television, being exposed to marketing messages, and the allure of these messages promising instant gratification, it is no surprise that parents, teachers and churches cannot compete.

In recent years special effort has been devoted to the so-called tweens, children aged eight to fourteen years. This new focus is not because tweens buy many of the goods marketed to them but because the advertisers hope to build brand loyalty that will pay off for decades:

> . . . car companies, airlines, hotels and financial services
> are competing with traditional kid marketers to establish a

relationship with young consumers. Initially targeted at teens, research and marketing programs are now seeking to understand and develop a relationship with younger consumers in the hope that their predisposition towards their brand will sway their purchasing decisions in the years to come. The result has been a dramatic increase in the number of advertising messages targeted at tweens . . .[29]

Brands have become an inseparable part of children's maturing consciousness. Nearly half the world's 8- to 12-year-old urban tweens say the clothes and brands they wear describe *who they are* and define their social status.[30] Lindstrom notes that tweens are exposed to more than 8000 brands a day and that they influence close to 60 per cent of all brand decisions made by their parents[31]:

> What has become clear is that more and more tweens define their worth, their role in the social hierarchy, their popularity, and their success by the brands they wear, eat and live with. . . . Functionality takes a back seat to the belief that along with ownership of a brand comes success and admiration . . . Tween tribes . . . have become active advocates for the brand.
>
> The dramatic change in the role of brands has been part of the advertising agencies' long-term goals. It was initially the advertisers who envisioned turning brand into a form of religion, to increase their sales. And it has worked.[32]

In fact, most children want to transcend the limitations of lifestyles manufactured by brands that are available to everyone. They want to achieve the new pinnacle of social success—celebrity.

They do not see fame as a reward for achievement: they see it as a state in itself. And, with the proliferation of celebrities whose fame owes nothing to talent or achievement, this is an accurate judgment. Lindstrom's worldwide survey of tweens found that more than half wanted to be famous, with children from India and the United States topping the list. In Australia, auditions for television shows that promise to create stars attract hundreds of thousands of young entrants, most of them with no particular talent. The desire for fame is a reflection of the broader trend in consumer societies to set ourselves external goals such as wealth, fame and physical attractiveness in place of intrinsic goals such as better relationships, self-development and participation in community.

Celebrity appears to be the opposite of what tweens fear most—rejection and social isolation. To gain acceptance they will go to extreme lengths. In a 1999 survey of tween and teenage girls, 46 per cent said they were unhappy with their bodies and 35 per cent said they would consider plastic surgery.[33] Being sexy is cool, and that's why even pre-pubescent girls are being sexualised. The Olsen sisters, who visited Australia in 2003, became famous as cute 5-year-old twins in a US sitcom before growing into pouting teenage entrepreneurs promoting sexy lingerie, including matching padded bras and panties, to their 6- to 12-year-old fans. If adults who are sexually attracted to children are called paedophiles, what do we call adults who set out to make children sexually attractive? Advertising executives.

Chapter 4
How much is enough?

*The trouble with the rat race is, even if you win,
you are still a rat.*

——attributed to Lily Tomlin

Wants and needs

Most people in consumer societies believe they need more money
than they have, no matter how wealthy they already are. Their
actions suggest they are convinced that more money means more
happiness. But when people reach the financial goals they have set
for themsleves they feel no happier. Instead of wondering whether
the yen for more money is the problem, they raise their threshold
of sufficiency. This is a vicious cycle. In part, it continues because
it is not the absolute level of income that affects our wellbeing but
the relative amount: it's no good being twice as rich if everyone else
is twice as rich too. Studies have shown that most people would
prefer an income of $50 000 if the average is $40 000 to an income
of $70 000 if the average is $100 000,[1] that is, most people would
rather be poorer, provided others are poorer still.

For 2004–05 the typical, or median, level of disposable income
for all families with children has been calculated at $50 500.[2] The

average disposable income is higher than the median. For the middle class, rising incomes in recent decades have been accompanied by an even faster rise in expectations about what is needed to live a decent life. Since aspirations always stay ahead of actual incomes, many people, who by any historical or international standard are wealthy, feel they are doing it tough. In late 2002 a Newspoll survey asked a representative sample of Australian adults whether they agreed or disagreed with the following statements:

- You cannot afford to buy everything you really need.
- You spend nearly all of your money on the basic necessities of life.[3]

Sixty-two per cent of Australians believe they cannot afford to buy everything they really need (see Figure 3). When we consider that Australia is one of the world's richest countries and that Australians today have incomes three times higher than in 1950, it is remarkable that so many people feel their incomes are inadequate. It is even more remarkable that almost half (46 per cent) of the richest 20 per cent of households in Australia—the richest people in one of the world's richest countries—say that they cannot afford to buy everything they really need.

Obviously, perceived needs change as incomes rise. When confronted with the question of whether they can afford everything they really need, people usually begin to think of the things that they would like to buy but cannot at present afford. The thoughts of wealthier people might turn to a new car, a fancier stove and a holiday in the sun; poor people would tend to think of a plumber to fix the leaking cistern, a new coat and money for a school excursion. When asked, wealthier people feel keenly their

FIGURE 3: Proportion of Australians agreeing that they cannot afford to buy everything they really need, by income group

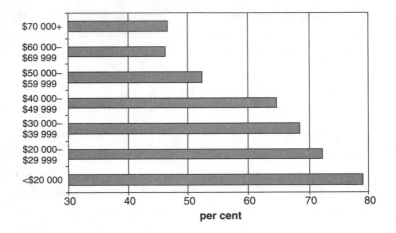

inability to afford what they feel they need, although on closer questioning they usually concede that they could do without an extension to their home, a vehicle upgrade or a holiday house. Their daily consciousness and their political attitudes are, however, driven by their sense of lack rather than a realistic appreciation of what they actually need—or, indeed, what they actually have. A decade ago 'everything you really need' would not have included a plasma-screen television, an ensuite bathroom, a phone that takes pictures and an outdoor kitchen, but for many people now it does. Pressured by their social milieu and advertising, people feel dissatisfied with what they have, so that what begins as a novelty becomes a 'must have'.

The confusion between wants and needs is at the heart of affluenza. When people see wants as needs, it is not surprising that two-thirds say they cannot afford everything they need. And their feelings of deprivation are real, since thwarted desire is transformed into a sense of deprivation. Of course, the purpose of the advertising industry is to convert perceived wants into perceived needs. Psychologists who treat people with compulsive shopping disorders often begin by helping them understand the difference between wants and needs.[4] Breaking the link is a vital stage in the therapeutic process, although in order to do it the therapist must dissolve a deeper association— between the acquisition of goods and a sense of self-worth, which is precisely the association advertisers labour to create. One group of psychologists works hard at trying to cure the disorders caused by another. Of course, it is a very unequal battle. A group called Debtors Anonymous uses a twelve-step program similar to that of Alcoholics Anonymous to break the nexus between wants and needs and teach their members to develop self-worth through other activities.

As noted, the respondents to the Newspoll survey were also asked whether they agreed or disagreed with the statement that they spend nearly all their money on the basic necessities of life. Fifty-six per cent of the respondents agreed (see Figure 4). More than a quarter of the wealthiest households in Australia believe they spend nearly all their money on the basic necessities of life.

All this suggests that Australian households—especially middle-income and wealthy households—have an inflated, perhaps grossly inflated, understanding of how much money they need to maintain a decent standard of living. It also confirms the view that as people become wealthier perceptions of the necessary consumption levels rise. This has profound implications for the conduct of politics in Australia.

FIGURE 4: Proportion of Australians agreeing that they spend nearly all their money on basic necessities, by income group

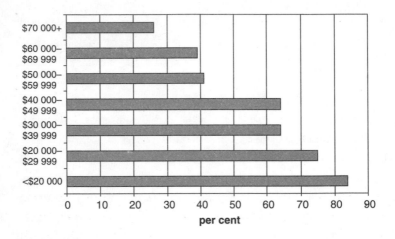

The delusion of growth

The results of the Australian survey have been replicated by surveys asking the same questions in the United States and the United Kingdom. Table 2 shows the results for the three countries, along with GDP per person in 2000.[5] In all cases, the top and bottom income groups each account for about 15 to 20 per cent of households. Incomes are those before tax.[6] The figures for the United Kingdom and Australia are surprisingly similar. Overall, six in ten people in each of the two countries say they cannot afford everything they really need. Nearly half of high-income households are dissatisfied with their incomes, while four out of five in the lowest income group are dissatisfied.

TABLE 2: Attitudes to needs, by income group—'You cannot afford to buy everything you really need'

Country	Total (%)	Lowest income group (%)	Highest income group (%)	GDP per person in 2000 (US$ PPP)
United Kingdom	61	79	46	23 509
Australia	62	79	47	25 693
United States	50	63	33	34 142

Note: PPP denotes purchasing power parity.

Australians and Britons appear, however, to be much more dissatisfied with their incomes than Americans, and this is the case at both the high and the low ends of the scale. Overall, half of Americans say they cannot afford to buy everything they really need, compared with six in ten Britons and Australians. Nearly half the wealthiest households in the United Kingdom and Australia say their incomes are inadequate, whereas only one-third of wealthy Americans take that view. Thus the proportion of 'suffering rich' in Australia is even higher than in the United States, which is widely regarded as the nation most obsessed with money.[7]

These survey results for Australia, the United Kingdom and the United States illustrate how we have become deluded by economic growth. It is now well established that once income levels reach a particular threshold further increases do not increase national happiness. As economists Bruno Frey and Alois Stutzer observe, 'In general, people in rich countries are clearly happier than are those in poor countries . . . But, for the rich countries, it does not seem that higher per capita income has any marked effect

FIGURE 5: Life satisfaction and income growth in Japan, 1958 to 1992 (NB: as income and life satisfaction are measured differently, here the values of each in 1958 have been set to 100. Thus the figure shows the values for subsequent years as percentage changes to the 1958 levels.)

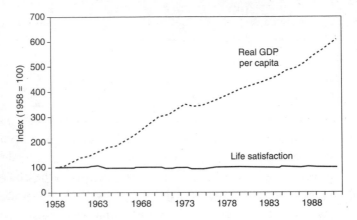

on happiness'.[8] When we plot measures of life satisfaction against income levels, life satisfaction increases with GDP per person up to about US$10 000 and then flattens out. Similarly, in rich countries increases in material standards of living are not associated with increases in life satisfaction. Figure 5 illustrates this for Japan. Similar figures could be drawn for other rich countries.

Real and imagined hardship

Recent studies help us understand the distinction between real and imagined hardship. One survey asked respondents whether they could afford to spend money on items such as annual holidays, a night out and hobbies.[9] By looking at specific behaviours, rather than general attitudes to financial circumstances, the survey elicited information on whether households actually go without necessities. With the exception of new clothes, the items in question—holidays away, eating out, having friends for a meal, and hobbies—cannot be considered physical necessities, although most would be regarded as essential to a reasonable standard of living in Australia today. Being able to participate in society is important to our wellbeing. As a child whose parents cannot afford to send them on a school excursion well knows, the inability to participate can be distressing.

In the case of items such as a week's holiday away, a night out once a fortnight and having friends around for a meal, the proportion of households saying they cannot afford them is relatively low, at 5 to 27 per cent, when compared with the general belief of 62 per cent of households that they cannot afford everything they really need or the 56 per cent who say they spend nearly all their income on the basic necessities of life. In other words, most Australians see items such as a week's holiday and a night out as 'needs' and 'basic necessities of life', at least for the middle class. Even among low-income households, only about 20 per cent say they have to do without special meals, new clothes and leisure activities, and 56 per cent of households in the lowest income group say they can afford a week's holiday each year.

Another study, by the Australian Bureau of Statistics,[10] found that on average 16 per cent of households could not pay their gas, electricity or telephone bills on time; this included 5 per cent of the wealthiest households. Although wealthy households can experience cash-flow problems that make them late in paying their bills, it would be fair to assume that the stress caused by the inability to pay bills on time is much greater among the poorest households. The same applies to the other items the Bureau of Statistics asked about. On the other hand, any household forced to pawn something, to go without meals or home heating or to seek assistance from a welfare organisation is experiencing genuine hardship. It is noteworthy, though, that even in the very lowest income group only about 10 per cent of households are so affected, and across the whole population perhaps only 3 or 4 per cent fall into this category. There could be other markers of genuine hardship that the Bureau's questions did not pick up, but even so it appears that a substantial majority of households in the lowest income group do not report hardship of this kind. As Bray notes, '. . . while lower-income households have, on average, higher levels of [financial] stress, many of these households experience no financial stress at all'.[11]

As one would expect, in the highest income group the incidence of genuine hardship is virtually zero. Yet nearly half of this group say they cannot afford to buy everything they really need. It is reasonable to conclude that, using any reasonable definition of 'needs' and 'basic necessities of life', a substantial majority of Australians who experience no real hardship believe they are 'doing it tough'. This might be seen as an unfortunate delusion on the part of the people concerned—except that the notion that large swathes of the Australian population are suffering some form of deprivation is one of the underlying suppositions of political debate and policy formulation in Australia. Among other things, it provides the basis for the political appeal of middle-class welfare and tax-cutting auctions at every federal election.

The debate about how to define a 'poverty line' has gone on in Australia for decades and has often been used as an excuse for doing nothing about poverty itself. Although we might not be able to agree on whether 5 or 15 per cent of Australians live in poverty, most people would agree that poverty is caused by unemployment, family breakdown, illness and disability. It should be apparent by now that the poverty debate is irrelevant for understanding affluenza: we might not know precisely where poverty ends and an adequate income begins but most of us know affluence when we see it.

When we pose the question 'How much is enough?' we are not concerning ourselves with the material shortages faced by the genuinely poor in Australia. The debate about how to define more clearly the poverty line is irrelevant to the lived experience of at least 80 per cent of Australians. In considering the definition of over-consumption, a lesson can, however, be learnt from attempts to define poverty: consensus is unlikely. It is no easier to determine whether buying a new car every two years or every four years signifies overconsumption than it is to determine whether an avocado is a basic food item or a luxury one. Trying to answer the question of how much is enough in material terms makes sense for people enduring material deprivation, but it is meaningless for middle- and high-income Australians. For the average Australian, asking how much income is enough is akin to asking how long is a piece of string.

When questions are too hard to answer it is often the case that we are asking the wrong question or thinking about the answer in the wrong way. To ask whether $40 000 a year is 'enough' misses the point. The problem of affluenza is not so much that we consume too much but that we measure our lives in terms of money and material things. Of course, any affluenza-afflicted Australian who seriously asks themselves whether they have enough will become aware that the more important question is 'What am I missing out on that money cannot buy?'

For some, the answer to this question might be 'nothing'. They might have a job they find rewarding, time to spend with their family and friends and time to pursue their passions—be they macramé, mountain climbing or saving the environment—and they might have learnt all they wish to learn about themselves, their society and the world. For such a person, pursuing a higher income in order to fulfil a material desire, if they still have one, could make sense.

But, for a person who finds their work stressful and unrewarding, who lacks the time or emotional energy to engage fully with their friends and family, who longs to spend more time on their hobbies or improving their mind, to ponder how much more money they need to be happy is a diversion—not a path towards happiness. The purpose of becoming rich, both as individuals and as a country, is to relieve ourselves of the burden of worrying about money, yet as our incomes have grown we seem to have become more preoccupied by our wealth, not less.

Part Two

The effects of affluenza

Chapter 5
Debt

Debt is the slavery of the free.

—Publilius Syrus, Roman aphorist, 42 BC

The debt binge

By some kind of financial alchemy, 'saving' has become what we do while we are spending. Bargain hunters can easily 'save' hundreds of dollars in the post-Christmas sales, but in order to save a great deal we need to max out our credit cards. Perverse as it sounds, we have been persuaded that the only way to save a lot is to borrow a lot. The idea of going without seems to be a relic of the age of piggy banks and anally retentive middle-class thrift.

In a society as deeply indebted as Australia, few people could dispute that saving a bit more money each week is a desirable objective. But, although almost everyone would agree they need to save more, most of them seem to think spending on discounted items is a good way to get started. Banks and financial institutions engaged in the marketing of debt have made billions by redefining the way Australians understand and use debt—a process that has resulted in radical changes to the way Australians spend, save and live. Debt is an essential element of the cycle of affluenza. It allows us to act on the desires created for us by the marketers, free of the banal constraint imposed by our incomes.

Young Australians have never known anything other than a deregulated financial market in which banks and new financial institutions fall over each other to lend them money. They have never had to be polite to a bank manager in order to secure a home loan. Instead of waiting a week to get an appointment with the bank, they expect the bank to visit them at home at a time that suits them. They have never had to wonder whether their application for a credit card will be successful. And most have never left work with a pay packet full of $20 bills to tide them over until the next pay day.

Perhaps the simplest definition of overconsumption is 'living beyond one's means'. For the past decade Australians have been on a credit binge. Each year we are borrowing ten times more for housing than we did fifteen years ago. In the decade to 2002, the ratio of household debt to average household income rose from 56 per cent to 125 per cent.[1] The average value of a mortgage rose from 2.8 times the average wage in 1994 to 4.2 times in 2004.[2] Spending on consumer goods is increasingly financed by credit card debt, which now exceeds $27 billion. The past decade has seen an extraordinary rise in personal debt: the amount doubled between 2001 and 2004 and increased fourfold between 1996 and 2004 (see Figure 6).

One of the consequences of the growth in consumer debt has been a sharp rise in personal bankruptcies. In 2003–04 nearly 21 000 Australians filed for personal bankruptcy; 74 per cent were consumers rather than businesses, and the most common age was between 22 and 44 years.[3] There are reports of 18-year-olds filing for bankruptcy, unable to pay mobile phone bills of $5000. The debt collection business is booming.[4] The proportion of people

FIGURE 6: Personal debt other than housing,
1990 to 2004

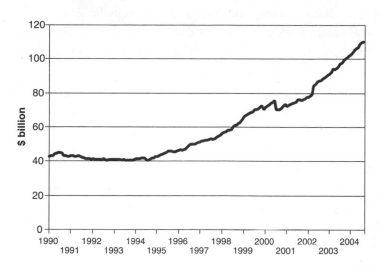

citing excessive use of credit as the reason for declaring themselves bankrupt has more than doubled, to over 21 per cent, in the past five years. To put this in perspective, the proportion of people citing excessive gambling or speculation as the cause of their bankruptcy is less than 3 per cent.[5]

Credit card debt, personal loans, car loans and store credit schemes are all growing rapidly—not to fund assets that will deliver benefits for years to come but to allow people to enjoy the 'lifestyle' they have been told they deserve. Expenditure on imported consumer goods rose by 60 per cent between 2000 and 2004.[6] Similarly, demand for imported luxury cars and overseas holidays has grown rapidly. Contrary to popular belief, the accumulation of consumer debt is not the result of poorer households being forced to borrow to cover living expenses: it is the result of wealthier households splashing out on luxuries. Households in the lowest income group (less than $20 000 a year) have the fewest debts and are much more likely than higher income households to have no debts at all.[7] Households with incomes of $40 000 to $60 000 are most likely to run up credit card debts,[8] which have been growing at an astonishing 20 per cent annually in recent years.[9]

In the 1950s and 1960s it was sometimes said that middle-class people saved because they embodied the values of thrift and prudence, while the working class was unable to delay gratification and spent as if there was no tomorrow. Whether that was true or not, the middle class today is no longer delaying gratification. They seem to want it all now and are willing to go into debt to get it. Low-income households, on the other hand, are less likely to carry large credit card debts. In part, this is because banks are less willing to extend them credit, but it is also because low-income earners tend to be more aware of the consequences of poor budgeting. Being evicted is much more upsetting than missing out on a holiday.

According to the Australian Consumers' Association, there has been a cultural change towards accepting high levels of personal debt: 'Three or five years ago only 25 per cent of people carried balances on their credit cards; the rest paid them off every month. Now 75 per cent of people are carrying balances'.[10] Credit card providers have been encouraging this trend, with the average credit card limit being increased each year so that it now exceeds $6000.[11]

Selling debt

Growth in consumer debt has partly been a consequence of the easy availability of credit. But that easy availability has been matched by intense demand. Attitudes to debt have changed dramatically since the early 1990s: consumer debt has moved from being a last resort to a first choice for a growing majority of the population. As noted earlier, for young people in particular debt is not a choice; it is the only way they know. Teenagers are aware that if they want to buy a car or to attend university they will need to accept taking on large amounts of debt. Saying 'no' to debt now means saying 'no' to the modern style of life.

Debt is no longer simply the result of persuading people to spend more than they earn: it has itself become a consumer good that needs to be marketed. Banks have used a number of strategies to encourage people to 'spend up big' on their credit cards. First, they increased fees and charges to encourage consumers to discard their cheque books and debit cards, which were linked to and constrained by their savings accounts. In many cases a fee is charged whenever a debit card is used, while consumers pay no transaction fees when they use their credit cards.

Having convinced people it's cheaper and more convenient to shop and pay bills with credit cards, the banks then set about increasing their customers' credit card limits, often without asking them. Safe in the knowledge that they have a large credit limit—'just for emergencies'—consumers are then able to begin the process of disconnecting their weekly spending from their weekly income. Accumulating a credit card bill of a few thousand dollars is neither difficult nor time consuming. Nor is it of concern to the banks. On the contrary: their best customers are the ones who carry their monthly balances forward. The minimum monthly repayment required by the banks is designed to maximise the amount of interest paid on the remainder, not to minimise the time needed to repay the loan. Banks profit from credit cards only if the cards are used in ways contrary to the banks' own advice. They never admit this, although in 2003 the CEO of one of Britain's biggest banks, Barclays, caused a storm by telling a parliamentary inquiry that he advises his children not to run up debts on their credit cards. 'I don't borrow on credit cards because it is too expensive,' said the boss of the bank that issues Britain's most successful credit card.[12]

The next step in encouraging people to splash out on their credit cards is to 'reward' them for all their hard spending. Free flights, fuel vouchers or a new toaster can all be 'earnt' simply by using your credit card to spend thousands of dollars. The idea that people can 'save up' for their holiday by spending plenty on their credit card to earn frequent flyer points might seem absurd, but that was the promise of a recent American Express advertising campaign. It informed consumers that, among other things, a pair of shoes was 'not just a pair of shoes, it's a step closer to that trip to Paris'. So we save by spending more. Debt is also made to appear more attractive by using other marketing devices—interest-free periods, no-deposit finance, no repayments for twelve months. All these schemes prop up the notion that consumers can have everything they want and can have it now.

The proliferation of loyalty schemes seems to have persuaded most Australians that they can obtain many of the things they want for free. Nothing is free. We pay higher grocery bills to fund discounts on petrol, higher plane fares to pay for frequent flyer programs, higher prices in department stores to fund fly-buy giveaways, and higher prices for everything else so that shopkeepers can pay the merchant fees for credit card transactions. The price of everything is higher so that we can be persuaded that much of what we want is free.

Debt delusions

Perhaps the most pervasive aspect of the marketing of debt has been dissemination of the idea that debt results in people acquiring more, rather than fewer, things. Credit allows people to bring forward their consumption, although the price of having more now is having much less in the future. For example, anyone who racked up a credit card debt of $5000 during 2004 will need to reduce their consumption expenditure by more than $11 000 in 2005 if they want to get back to where they were. That's right: if your credit card debt grew by $5000, then to get back on an even keel you need to factor in three separate hits to your 'lifestyle'. First, you can't keep spending $5000 more than you earn each year, so you are going to need to reduce your weekly expenditure by about $100 a week. Second you are going to have to repay that $5000 extra that you spent in 2004. That's going to mean you have to reduce your spending by a further $100 a week. And, finally, you are going to have to pay back the interest and, at up to 18 per cent for a credit card, that's likely to come to more than $1000.

Of course, you don't have to pay it all back next year; you don't even have to pay any of it back. The banks are very happy for you to keep 'saving' money at the sales and spending more than you earn—as long as you keep paying them their interest. Although there have been many complaints about bank fees, the reality is that most of the banks' profits come from interest payments.

It is true that a person who is willing to save will always end up with more money and, in turn, have the potential to buy more things. But neither the banks nor the retailers are keen for us to begin conserving our money. They might benefit when we eventually spend our savings, but thrift hurts them now. Retailers know that the longer we think about a purchase the less likely we are to make it. Calm consideration often means no sale. That's why they love the 'doorbuster' sales. What better way to sell the things no one wanted last year than to turn it into a competition? People's fear of 'missing out on a bargain' seems to be much stronger than their fear of wasting their money on something they don't really need. In addition, when people have to pull cash from their wallet they often stop and think about the need for the purchase, so, perhaps unsurprisingly, retailers are now working on technologies that will allow credit card details to be read without the customer even taking the card out of their wallet as they pass through the checkout. All we will need to do is walk into a shop, take what we want from the shelves, and walk out. It will be like shoplifting without the fear.

One of the most surprising and profitable trends in Australian banking in recent years has been individuals' willingness to lend money to themselves and pay their bank up to 18 per cent for the privilege: an increasing number of Australians have chosen to carry credit card balances of thousands of dollars while at the same time holding a few thousand dollars in a fixed-term deposit or other special savings account. Of the $27.8 billion outstanding on credit cards in August 2004, interest was being paid on $19.5 billion—about three-quarters.[13] Even though most savings accounts pay little or no interest, and most credit cards charge interest rates of 15 to 20 per cent, it seems that many Australians will pay the bank in order to avoid admitting they are suffering from affluenza.

If consumers behaved in accordance with the economists' 'rational' script, they would withdraw any spare money in their savings accounts and repay as much credit card debt as possible. That way, they would minimise the amount of interest they pay.

It is not surprising to learn that not all consumers behave in the way assumed by the economic rationalists, but it is nevertheless interesting to think about why they are unwilling to do so. It seems that people do not like to admit, to themselves or their friends, that they have not been able to save any money. By carrying a credit card debt and a positive balance in a savings account, they can effectively 'rent' the feeling that they have some savings. Such self-deception is a symptom of chronic affluenza, and it creates a bonanza for the banks.

Not long ago, paying off the mortgage on the family home quickly was a common dream. A more recent dream appears to be to extend both the size of the mortgage and the period required to pay it off by borrowing against the home to fund a better 'lifestyle'. One advertisement for home equity loans declares:

> So whether you own your home entirely, or it is partly mort-gaged, the equity in your home is a valuable asset which may be used to help you achieve your goals.
> For example, you could use your equity to finance a loan:
> - for home improvements or extensions
> - to buy a new car or boat
> - to take a well deserved holiday
> - to pay for your or your children's education
> - for business and investment
> - for any other purpose.[14]

Instead of focusing on how much we still owe on our houses, we have been taught to focus on how much of our houses we already own. Equity in a house is regarded as 'dead money' unless we start 'using' it. Borrowing against a house to buy an expensive item can be cheaper than taking out a personal loan, but the problem with home equity loans is not their lower interest rates: it is the way they are marketed as a means to 'have it all'. These loans, which now account for about 15 per cent of all home loans, are often used to create a desire for new purchases. The message from the lenders is that with home equity loans you don't need to wait for anything:

> If you've got plans for your home, there's no need to wait. We can help you get the money to make it happen today. More than just money for home improvements, we can also help you with money for nearly any purpose. No matter what you need it for, from a holiday to a car, we make getting the money you need easy.[15]

Our dwindling ability to think carefully about what we really need and whether we can afford to buy what we want lies at the heart of our debt problems. For all the recent talk of improving our 'financial literacy', Australians are increasingly prone to financial stupidity. People who are permanently in debt exist in a 'money coma'—a state of vagueness and confusion about their financial circumstances. One of the steps to recovery from uncontrolled debt is to be very clear about how much you owe and how you can manage your financial life without incurring more debts, yet retailers and consumer lenders work hard to undermine our resolve and confuse us about what taking on debts actually means.

A first step taken by people who join Debtors Anonymous is to admit their powerlessness over debt and to acknowledge they have lost control of their lives. Unlike alcoholics, who can avoid situations that tempt them to drink, debt addicts cannot reasonably remove themselves from the temptations they constantly face to go into debt. Debt and overspending are everywhere. Although Debtors Anonymous helps people who have lost themselves to debt, in the last ten to fifteen years the symptoms of chronic indebtedness have to some degree affected most of us.

The ballooning of consumer debt has had far-reaching cultural and social impact. Australians are increasingly seduced by the argument that they deserve to be rewarded at every turn and that they deserve their rewards now. As more and more individuals accept such a view of the world, the pressure on people who resist increases. While new cars, new clothes and expensive watches are highly visible, large credit card debts, long work hours and relationship stresses are more easily concealed—at least for a time.

Our perceptions are influenced by people's visible behaviours rather than the less visible consequences, and the fact that many consumers are increasingly dependent on debt finance is helping to raise the apparent 'standard of living' by which the rest of the population compares itself. The upward spiral of desire, debt and consumption has fuelled massive growth in retail spending but appears to have delivered little benefit for national wellbeing. However, when even the banks become reluctant to lend any more money and the borrow–spend nexus is finally broken, it is likely that individual and national wellbeing will fall substantially. The credit card is to someone suffering from affluenza what a bottle shop is to an alcoholic—a disaster wrapped in paradise.

The national debt

In October 2004 the Australian Bureau of Statistics reported that the total wealth of Australians had reached $5 trillion, or $250 000 per person. This represents an 18 per cent increase over the preceding year and a doubling of wealth over the preceding seven years, most of it a result of the boom in house prices. Although for the majority of people the increase in their wealth is on paper only (because when they decide to cash in the world could be very different), they have nevertheless felt wealthier and have increased their spending accordingly. Economists call this the 'wealth effect'.

At the national level, the increase in consumer debt has been accompanied by a decline in savings. In 1975 Australian households saved 16.4 per cent of their after-tax income; now they save minus 3.2 per cent, that is, we 'dissave', despite the fact that average real incomes have nearly doubled.[16] One consequence of the national credit card binge has been a dramatic increase in the level of national debt. In 1996, when the then Opposition leader, John Howard, drove the 'foreign debt truck' through marginal seats during the election campaign, national debt stood at $194 billion and reducing it was seen as an economic imperative, with Mr Howard pledging to do so as a matter of urgency. By the time of the 2004 election campaign, the national debt had doubled to $393 billion and the current account deficit was adding to our foreign debt at record levels, yet the Howard Government campaigned on the strength of its 'economic management'. In an interview in the lead-up to that election, Prime Minister Howard refused to renew his commitment to reducing national debt. What happened? Why is it that huge debts no longer matter?

Some level of national debt—the difference between the amount of money Australians owe lenders in other countries and the amount borrowers in other countries owe us—is not inherently bad. Australia is a relatively young country that has experienced rapid population growth in the last 50 years. It is understandable that money might need to be borrowed to fund investments such as roads, railways and electricity infrastructure. As anyone who has borrowed to buy a house knows, there is nothing irresponsible about borrowing money in order to buy something that will deliver long-term benefits, so long as the money is invested in ways that improve the borrower's capacity to repay it. For example, borrowing to buy a house is generally a wise move because we then avoid paying rent and save a lot of tax if we enjoy a capital gain.

But the rapid growth in Australians' borrowing is not the result of any rapid increase in government, corporate or personal investment: it is primarily the result of increased spending on imported consumer goods. The economic debate has 'moved on' from worrying too much about national debt and current account deficits, but the Australian economy will probably pay a high price for the consumer debt binge of the last ten years—the result of the change in consumer behaviour from 'pre-saving' (saving up to buy something) to 'post-saving' (buying something on credit then paying it off over time). We can only make this transition once. In the end, we have to pay off our debts with the same income stream.

The political and economic arguments in favour of reduced government spending asserted that government deficits both increase national debt and draw funds away from the private sector. This 'twin deficits' theory was used to argue that the private sector is in a better position than governments to make spending decisions and—although little evidence to support that claim was ever presented—it became an article of faith. The experience of the past decade, in which much of our foreign debt has gone to fund the consumer binge rather than investment in long-lasting productive assets, is likely to result in a revision of this view.[17] As government expenditure on schools, hospitals, public transport and aged care has slowed, private expenditure on plasma-screen televisions, mobile phones that take photographs, and water features for drought-affected gardens has boomed. Public investment in social infrastructure would have continued to provide benefits long after plasma-screen televisions have been replaced by home theatres and water features have become as passé as vinyl armchairs and orange carpet.

When growth in consumer goods, rather than investment in long-lived assets, is the driving force behind rising debt the problem is exacerbated. Just as individuals who have been living beyond their means must eventually face reality, drastically lower their spending and start repaying their debts, so too must the national economy. Retail sales of imported appliances cannot drive economic growth forever. When most Australian consumers finally switch from borrowing to repaying, the economy-wide consequences could be severe.

Chapter 6
Overwork

I owe, I owe, it's off to work I go.

———bumper sticker

The laid-back Aussie?

A Sydney merchant banker who worked very long hours was persuaded by his wife to take a day off work to spend some time with his teenage son David. David pined for his dad's attention, but he was always too busy. Nevertheless, the banker took a day off and they spent a magical day sailing. Although never repeated, David stored it in his memory as the wonderful day he spent alone with his father.

A few years later the merchant banker died suddenly of a heart attack and David, now in his twenties, found his father's work diaries when going through his things. He opened one up to the date they went sailing. His father had written: 'Complete waste of a day'.

———story told to a person researching downshifting

Many Australians still see themselves as living in the land of the long weekend. But for most Australian workers having a sickie, knocking off for smoko and taking long lunches are things of the past. During the last twenty years there has been a gradual but relentless increase in working time in most organisations—so much so that Australians now work the longest hours in the developed world: 1855 hours a year compared with 1835 in the United States and an OECD average of 1643.[1] Our first placing is even more noteworthy for the fact that Australia has the second-highest proportion of part-time employees (27 per cent) in the workforce, something that acts to drag down the average.[2]

Only 28 per cent of employees work a standard week of between 35 and 40 hours.[3] This is partly because of the growing importance of part-time and casual work but also because of the fact that 42 per cent of men in full-time jobs work more than 45 hours a week (the equivalent of a nine-hour day), more than 30 per cent work more than 50 hours a week (a ten-hour day) and nearly 15 per cent work more than 60 hours a week (a twelve-hour day).[4] The proportion of men working these long hours has grown substantially in the past twenty years. Women are less likely to work long hours, but they are catching up fast: between 1978 and 2004 the proportion of women working more than 45 hours a week more than doubled, from 12 per cent to over 25 per cent, and in the same period the proportion of women working more than 50 hours a week doubled, to more than 15 per cent.[5]

There is no doubt that in the past twenty years Australians have been spending more time at work. It is possible, however, that this situation is simply a benefit of deregulation, whereby a longstanding desire on the part of workers to work for longer can now be achieved. Although information about the desire for long hours is limited, the results of one large survey suggest people do not want to work long hours. The survey found that 54 per cent of people working more than 48 hours a week would prefer to work fewer hours.[6] Obviously, some workers like to work long hours because they find their jobs fulfilling, but these 'workophiles' should be distinguished from workaholics, who are driven by inner compulsions; victims of affluenza, who work longer to have more money; and workers who fear the sack if they ask to work reasonable hours.

Discussions of overwork have typically centred on the length of the average working day. There is another important dimension to overwork—the number of days worked each year. It is widely believed that Australians benefit from a large number of public holidays, but international comparisons prove otherwise. The Australian Capital Territory and all the states except New South Wales have eleven public holidays a year (including the eight national public holidays); the Northern Territory and New South Wales have ten. Australian public holiday entitlements are around the European Union average but well below the fifteen days enjoyed by the Japanese and the twelve to fourteen enjoyed by the Italians, Spanish and Portuguese.[7]

Full-time employees in Australia are entitled to a minimum of four weeks' annual leave. No European Union country has fewer paid annual holidays than Australia: workers average more than five weeks of annual leave, while those in Germany and the Netherlands enjoy six. Besides, millions of Australians have found that an entitlement to four weeks' annual leave does not necessarily translate into actually having four weeks off. In 2002 only 39 per cent of full-time employees used up their four-week entitlement. Failure to take four weeks' leave was higher amongst men (60 per cent) than women (53 per cent) and higher among respondents aged 35 to 49 years (60 per cent) compared with those aged 50 to 59 years (48 per cent).[8] Many cited pressure of work as the main obstacle to taking leave.

Annual holidays are an important component of total hours worked during the course of a year. Going without four weeks' holiday leave is equivalent to working an additional three hours a week. Holidays provide benefits that are qualitatively different from those flowing from a shorter working week. After a holiday, few people return to work determined to work longer hours and see less of their family. Holidays allow families to spend time together, to travel to see friends and extended families, and to unwind and reassess their priorities. Holidays offer the emotional composure required to diagnose affluenza, and perhaps find a cure for it.

Yes, billions of people in developing countries work long hours with few holidays in order to subsist, but prosperity was supposed to deliver us from this. And for several decades that was the trend. In fact, in the 1970s, with the postwar boom more than a quarter of a century old, policy makers began to think for the first time about the impact of steadily increasing labour productivity and rising incomes. The problem on their minds was 'What will Australians do with all their leisure?' At the time, nobody suspected the answer would be to work longer and longer hours to pay for bigger and bigger houses filled with more and more things.

Like influenza, affluenza can spread rapidly through the cubicles and corridors of the modern airconditioned workplace. Increasingly competitive and hierarchical workplaces promote the sort of self-doubt and one-upmanship that cause people to redefine their life goals. An individual might start their first job relatively immune to the siren song of conspicuous consumption and the long hours of work this often entails. But they might quickly find that, in order to progress in the workplace, they must work and behave in ways that the organisation demands of them. After five years of working long hours, losing touch with friends and family, and mixing entirely with people immersed in the work–spend culture, it is likely that some individuals, if only out of uncertainty about what else to do, will acquire the materialist motivations that appear to make the long hours 'worth it'.

Despite the constant changes to the Australian industrial relations system since the time of Federation, the changes in the most recent period have been described as 'the most systematic and far reaching'.[9] While proponents of labour market deregulation often promote the virtue of increased flexibility, it is this same 'virtue' that has drawn the most criticism from others. The problem facing both policy makers and the public at large is that the advantages highlighted by one group are the disadvantages highlighted by another. Some employees have benefited from greater flexibility and the increased availability of part-time work, but millions of others have experienced increased work intensity, longer hours and reduced security as a result of labour market deregulation. Deregulation has increased stress levels—from having too much work, not enough work or not enough job security. Such a climate is conducive to the spread of affluenza: the overworked and overpaid spend to compensate for their lost time; the underworked are tempted to engage in retail therapy to spend their blues away.

Deferred happiness syndrome

Affluenza is a form of self-deception; it comes about as a result of the stories we tell ourselves. One of the stories Australians tell themselves could be called 'deferred happiness syndrome'.[10] A large number of people persist with life situations that are difficult, stressful and exhausting in the belief that the sacrifice will pay off in the longer term. Focus groups reveal that the sacrifices many identify are centred on their relationships with family and friends, while others believe they are forgoing activities that would make their lives fulfilling—the things they had 'always wanted to do'. Some endure many years of stress, sometimes resulting in ill health, in order to pursue the long-term dream of a 'happy' retirement.

There are various motivations for deferring happiness in these ways. Some people aspire to a more extravagant lifestyle, as reflected in rapidly increasing house prices. The desire to stay in the race leads many to work longer and harder, often at the cost of other aspects of their wellbeing. Other people feel a need to accumulate as much as they can in preparation for their retirement; this is especially prevalent among men in their 40s and 50s. Participants in focus group discussions return to this theme repeatedly. Some workers are stuck in demanding jobs because they are fearful of the consequences if they were to change. They become inured to the stresses and pressures—perhaps until a health problem or a crisis at work or at home forces them to think about alternatives.

The impact of long hours on family relationships can be severe, with many workers feeling they are neglecting their partners and children. In a Newspoll survey, 80 per cent of respondents agreed that people are spending too much time working and too little with their families and friends.[11] Nine out of ten believe family is more important than work, yet many overworked parents are spending less time with their children. There is widespread recognition that when parents work long hours their children suffer: 81 per cent of men and 70 per cent of women say children are better off at home with a parent. A researcher at Queensland University of Technology found that the wives of workers who are often away from home for extended periods experience higher levels of anxiety, stress and depression than the general population.[12] Called 'intermittent husband syndrome', the condition puts marriages under pressure because the cycle of parting and reunion often causes a recurring crisis. Teenage children are also more likely to be affected by parents' frequent absences because of excessive work commitments. Some men feel guilty about neglecting their children while they work long hours,[13] but they also feel a need to 'provide for their families' and are torn between conflicting goals.

How many Australians suffer from deferred happiness syndrome? A national Newspoll survey in 2004 asked whether respondents agreed or disagreed with the statement 'Your work means you currently neglect your relationships with family and friends, but you plan to make up for it in later years'.[14] People who say the statement describes them are deemed to have the syndrome, and Figure 7 shows that this applies to 30 per cent of full-time workers in Australia. Men are a little more prone to contracting the syndrome than women, and workers with children are more likely to contract it (34 per cent) than workers without (27 per cent). The syndrome is also somewhat more common among workers aged more than 50 years (35 per cent), which is perhaps explained by older workers' focus on their retirement income. Not surprisingly, workers from households with incomes greater than $60 000 a year seem to be more prone to contracting the syndrome (32 per cent of them are afflicted) compared with workers from households with incomes less than $30 000 (only 15 per cent are afflicted). This may reflect a greater preoccupation with financial security on the part of wealthier households. Many

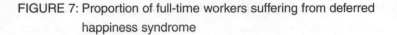

FIGURE 7: Proportion of full-time workers suffering from deferred happiness syndrome

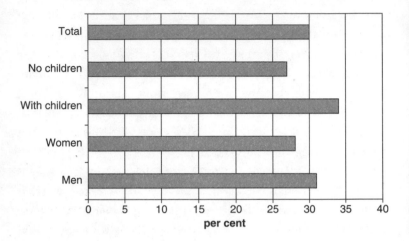

middle-aged and older workers 'live for their retirement', imagining a time of extended bliss that is worth major sacrifices in the preceding decades. Superannuation fund advertisements showing couples in their golden years walking hand in hand on the beach exploit this image, yet many retirees find that after a lifetime of long working hours they have neither the relationship nor the living skills to realise the dream.

Working ourselves sick

Health

The Japanese workplace is notorious for *karoshi*—death by overwork. A study of Japanese employees who had died from cardiovascular attack found that over two-thirds had worked more than 60 hours a week, 50 overtime hours a month or more than half of their fixed holidays before their attack.[15] In Australia, too, many employees are working themselves towards an early death. A study commissioned by the Federal Government explored the effect of overwork on employees and found that longer working hours are linked to lifestyle illnesses such as obesity, alcoholism and cardio-vascular disease.[16]

The most obvious consequence of extended working hours is their effect on the amount and quality of sleep and the associated reduction in alertness and increase in fatigue. Given the high pro-portion of employees now working more than 50 hours a week, the fact that the effects of a reduction in sleep can occur once an employee exceeds 48 hours of work a week[17] is a cause for concern. More Australians die in their workplaces than in car accidents each year. And, as with car accidents, it is the young who are most likely to be killed. One study found a significant increase in fatal workplace accidents beyond the ninth hour of work.[18] Addition-ally, the increase in car accidents attributed to driver fatigue ('microsleeps') could be a consequence of a larger number of exhausted workers behind the wheel.

But the effects of overwork are not just physical. One study found links between long hours and certain mental disorders—among them substance abuse and a tendency to anxiety and depres-sion, headaches and sleep disturbances resulting from both the long hours of work and the substance abuse.[19] Researchers have also examined the effects of extended working hours on preg-nancy and miscarriage. The findings suggest an increased risk of preterm births for women engaged in shift work or hours of work beyond 40 hours a week. Research from the United States also shows that long work hours cause reduced foetal growth and low birthweight babies.[20]

Although long hours leave workers sick and tired, there is a market in helping to solve that problem. Television advertisements for vitamins ask whether we are 'feeling 100 per cent' and suggest that it is a shortage of vitamin A—rather than working 60 hours a week—that might be making us feel run-down. Paracetamol advertisements depict unstoppable automatons taking rapid-action pain-relief capsules. In doing so, they sell not only a pill but also the belief that when we feel sick we should 'soldier on'. We shouldn't. We should stay at home in bed to recover and not spread our ailments through the airconditioning at work. The nation that once defined itself in terms of the sickie is now, on the whole, afraid to take one. A few organisations accept that workers need a 'mental health day off' to combat accumulating stress, but many others are characterised by 'presenteeism'—'the feeling that one must show up for work even if one is too sick, stressed, or distracted to be productive; the feeling that one needs to work extra hours even if one has no extra work to do'.[21]

Pharmaceutical companies are investing billions in developing new treatments for heart disease, stress, anxiety and obesity. Instead of working longer hours to afford these new treatments, society would benefit more from reducing overwork and workplace stress. Who would have guessed that being rich would be so bad for our health?

Communities

You will never know your neighbours are there.

——real estate advertisement

It is hard to coach your kids' soccer team after school if you don't get home from work until 7 p.m. It is even harder if you have to work every weekend. Working long and irregular hours does not just cause accidents and make us sick and tired: it breaks down the bonds that hold our communities together. The rise of twelve-hour shifts is having a dramatic impact on some communities:

> You can see the difference in the town that the 12-hour shifts have done. Like sport, this town has produced some of the best sportsmen . . . Like we've got good hockey players, good rugby league players, good golfers, cricketers, stuff like that . . . But as soon as the 12-hour shifts started again, it just killed it. Like now they struggle to get a football team, where at one time we were putting three teams on the paddock.[22]

As well as stripping away the time people would generally have to devote to community activities, overwork seems to shape people's mindsets in such a way that they feel their community is something they must protect themselves from rather than a resource from which they can draw and to which they can contribute. When hours become precious, people tend to hoard them. A man who had previously done four to eight hours a week of voluntary work had this to say:

> We find now we are doing things for ourselves, when before we were doing things for other people . . . There's a real debate, a real conscious issue within yourself over that. It becomes a bit of a struggle and you do get yourself worked up in that sense . . . as a consequence of working these unpaid hours.[23]

Community involvement takes time, but it also has the potential to provide great benefits for the individuals involved. Because long hours force people to retreat from community involvement—whether it be playing in the local footy team or helping out with meals on wheels—'leisure time' has become more commodified or more lonely, or both.

In general, involvement in community activities is a low-cost, or no-cost, way to spend leisure time. As people retreat from these activities they are likely to spend more money on eating out, renting movies or going away for the weekend—pursuits that cost much more than doing some volunteer work with friends or attending a post-match sausage sizzle. Withdrawal from community also reinforces the tendency among people who work long hours to mix almost exclusively with their workmates. There is nothing wrong with forming friendships with work colleagues, but problems do arise when individuals are unable to gain an external perspective on their work culture and the hours they are working. Community activity facilitates much broader mixing across socio-economic groups. Although hierarchies can exist in community and sporting groups, they are less likely to be based solely on income and profession. The broader an individual's social network the less likely it is that they will see themselves at the bottom of the pecking order, because the definition of 'success' will differ widely across different organisations.

Overwork's corrosive effect on communities is another vector for affluenza. Community ties offer people low-cost entertainment and a broader perspective on the appropriateness of excessive work and overconsumption. A commitment to community activities can also give us the reason we need to leave work on time. Conspicuous consumption is likely to be less important to people who are well known in their communities because more people will know what they are really like and will respect and admire them. It is necessary to judge someone by the type of car in their driveway only if you have never actually met them.

Relationships

'Sometimes you come home and you are so tired you can't eat. It affects your moods, really ratty, really bad tempered and short tempered and you really run on a short wick.'[24] There aren't many Australians who believe that working long hours is good for their relationships. In fact, three-quarters of the population say that spending more time with family and friends would increase their happiness.[25] People might tell themselves the money they earn is helping them build a stable future or they might think it helps them provide for their children, but most see long work hours as a means to an end rather than an end in themselves. Working long hours can be a costly way to build relationships:

> I miss him very much and I get very angry about that . . . He's in a constant state of jet lag. His intolerance is very high because he is tired. He has a vision of coming home to a Brady Bunch family because he misses us so much and we can never match that. And because he's tired, he's intolerant and that leads to a lot of conflict and resentment on my part, I think 'I waited all effing week for you to get back and this is what you . . .' you know and he thinks 'Why am I here? I'm just a visitor in my own home'.[26]

Long work hours do not just separate families: they also help define the time families spend together. A parent who regularly walks in the door at 8 p.m. is unlikely to be able to provide the same quality of time with their spouse or children as one who arrives home at 5.30 p.m. Weekends will probably not be a time of relaxed togetherness when a family member has just finished a 60-hour week. For most, the calculus is simple: beyond a certain point, the more energy put into work the less energy there is for the family.

It must be asked of those suffering deferred happiness syndrome whether the long hours are justified by the benefits family members receive from the additional income. The only study of its type in Australia found that the answer most commonly given by the children affected is 'no'.[27] The study found that the majority of young people want more time with their parents, rather than more money from increased hours of parental work. Interestingly, this was the case for children in all family structures—dual earner, single–earner couple households and single–parent earner households.[28]

In households where a single earner (typically the father) works long hours in a demanding job children's preference for time with their absent parent is especially strong. These households have been called 'hyper-breadwinner' households. The preference for more time with absent parents appears just as strong in households with a mother at home as in dual-earner households. Parents might think they can share the work and care tasks, but children do not seem to see it this way. Regardless of the amount of extra money one parent can bring in, children want the time and attention of both their parents. Barbara Pocock calls this 'parent-specific time-hunger', and in the vast majority of cases this means children want to spend more time with their fathers. As one child put it, 'He's just not there, and you start to miss him after a while . . . Sometimes he has to miss things and he doesn't like that. He's done it since I was a little baby and he's missed all kinds of things, like when I was a baby and things like that. He's missed out on lots of things and he doesn't like it'.[29]

A final anecdote symbolises the emotional cost of the modern conflict between the demands of work and the ties of family. A young man working in the highly competitive finance sector was called in by his bosses to discuss the progress of his work. After a few minutes he broke down in tears, confessing that he had been working so hard that he had not once seen his 10-month-old daughter awake.

Chapter 7
Wasteful consumption

I want to be effluent, Mum. Effluent.

———Kim from ABC TV's *Kath and Kim*

The psychology of buying

People afflicted by affluenza have an insatiable appetite for more things. Although our desire might have no bounds, our capacity to use things is limited: there is only so much we can eat, wear and watch, and a house has only so many rooms we can usefully occupy. The difference between what we buy and what we use is waste.

Ostensibly, we go to the shops to buy the things we need—or, at least, we go to buy things we hope will make us more contented. Increasingly, Australians go shopping for the thrill of the purchase, rather than for the anticipated pleasure to be gained from owning or using something. As one marketing strategist puts it, 'We are beyond satisfying basic demands and we have moved to a tertiary level where consumption becomes leisure. Even the stores that appear to be for basic needs are really about leisure'.[1] Shopping today is often done for 'mood enhancement'—even though retail therapy has short-lived benefits and is more costly than Prozac. This means that waste is not a troublesome by-product of what we consume but a consequence of the strategies we adopt to find meaning in our lives through shopping. Instead of finding more effective ways to fill the inner void, we end up digging and filling holes in the landscape. Dealing with ever-growing piles of waste is not an engineering problem: it is a psychological and social one.

Much of our consumption behaviour is designed to bridge the gap between our ideal selves and our actual selves. The advertisers work to persuade us that we can construct an ideal self out of the brands they promote. The trouble is that when we buy something to satisfy our ideal self we often find that the actual self gets in the way. We buy cooking ingredients so that we can turn our kitchens into founts of exotic foods, but we are too tired or too lacking in motivation to prepare more than one special meal. And the kitchen appliances we were going to use to effect the culinary transformation languish in the bottom of the cupboard, while the special utensils sit untouched in the third drawer down. We learn it is not really feasible to fit a size 14 body into a size 10 dress. We realise that making proper use of the exercise bike we just bought requires a commitment of 30 minutes a day and a willingness to pedal through pain and soreness, so the exercise bike gathers dust in the shed, next to the bicycle. The children have left home, but we buy a bigger house so that we can comfortably accommodate all those guests and grandchildren, and the spare rooms remain empty for most of the year.

Of course, the marketing industry is devoted to persuading us to buy things we don't need—and often to buy things we don't want. But it is not just the marketing industry: it is the entire economic and political system that conspires to breakdown any resistance to buying. If we fail to keep spending, dire warnings are issued. An article in the *Wall Street Journal* in 2004 lamented Europeans' unwillingness to spend unnecessarily and their penchant for electing governments that introduce laws to restrict retail hours and the use of credit cards: 'Western Europe has only 0.27 credit cards per person, compared with 2.23 in the US. [In Australia we have 0.75.] . . . Moreover, many affluent Europeans just do not want to spend their free time shopping'.[2]

US leaders have characterised shopping as a patriotic duty. The CEO of one of Germany's largest makers of household items has complained, 'People have an urge to spend nothing'.[3] Europeans' reluctance to spend money on goods they don't want has become so alarming that in 2004 the head of the European Central Bank instructed Europeans, 'It is time for you to consume'. No such urging has been required for Australian consumers.

These pressures have the effect of making us buy many things we don't really want. And we are embarrassed when we succumb, so we adopt strategies to conceal from ourselves and others just how much we spend on things we don't use. We put things away and tell ourselves we will use them later. We hoard things because we feel guilty about throwing them out. Many compulsive shoppers say they have cupboards full of shopping bags they never got around to opening. The self-storage industry allows us to assuage our guilt by storing things away, telling ourselves we will eventually make use of them. The only beneficiaries of our wasteful behaviour are the charities that recycle some of our redundant items and the retailers that sold them to us.

Waste does little for our wellbeing, but it is crucial to the health of the economic system, which is why many business groups are implacably opposed to measures designed to tackle waste. While governments urge us to 'reduce, re-use and recycle' manufacturers and marketers of consumer goods spend billions persuading us to do otherwise. Continued opposition to the imposition of a levy on plastic bags, for example, is based on the fear that once consumers take their own bags to the shops they will begin to think about their needs rather than stroll around the aisles buying things needlessly.[4] Having decided how many bags to take to a shop, consumers have effectively decided how much they will take home. Taking their own shopping bags helps to insulate them from impulse buying.

How much do we waste?

A recent survey has for the first time revealed the extent of wasteful consumption in Australia and our attitudes to spending money on things we never use.[5] Virtually all Australians admit to wasting money buying things they never use—food, clothes, shoes, CDs, books, exercise bikes, cosmetics, blenders, and much more. Although nearly two-thirds of Australians say they cannot afford to buy everything they really need, they admit to spending a total of $10.5 billion every year on goods they do not use. That is an average of $1226 for each Australian household—more than the total government spending on universities, pharmaceuticals or roads. If Australians curtailed their fruitless spending, in two years they could pay off most of their credit card debts.[6]

What do we waste our money on? Most of it is spent on uneaten food, including fresh fruit and vegetables, takeaway food and home-cooked leftovers. We threw away more than $5.2 billion worth of food and drink in 2004 (see Figure 8).

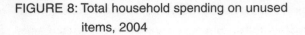

FIGURE 8: Total household spending on unused items, 2004

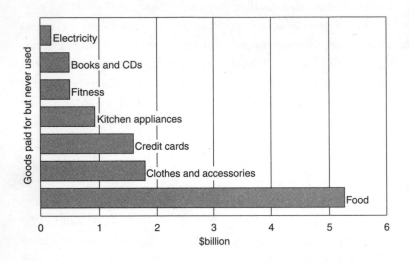

Thirty-five per cent of Australians admit to discarding more than $500 a year in fresh food alone, with one in seven households (14 per cent) throwing away more than $2500 worth.

The idea that we should eat large quantities of fresh fruit and vegetables, prepare regular meals at home and take our leftovers to work each day for lunch is attractive. But the reality for many is that they are too busy, tired or disorganised to behave as they know they 'should'. The marketers understand this, and our desire to live up to an ideal self is their greatest asset.

Of course, waste is not confined to the kitchen. We waste billions on clothes and shoes we never wear, exercise equipment we never use, and CDs we never listen to. Uneaten food quickly finds its way to the garbage bin, but these items can be stored for years, so most houses have cupboards, or even rooms, where unused stuff is hidden away. For many, the idea of a 'spring clean' now has more to do with disposing of the year's accumulated paraphernalia than with dusting and carpet cleaning.

We also waste money on services and things such as unused sports club memberships and interest on credit card debts that are not paid on time. The result is less damaging to the environment, but it harms individuals and communities. The disparity between how we think we should behave and how we actually behave provides the explanation for the amount of money wasted on gym memberships and exercise equipment. The study reveals that in 2004 Australians spent more than half a billion dollars on gym memberships and exercise equipment that they rarely or never use.

The extent of wasteful consumption varies according to the characteristics of households. Rich households waste more than households with modest incomes. For example, households with incomes between $20 000 and $40 000 throw out an average of $306 worth of fresh food each year, whereas households with incomes over $100 000 discard over $520 worth (see Figure 9). And, while 41 per cent of respondents from households with incomes of less than $20 000 said they wasted no fresh food, only 11 per cent of respondents from households earning over $100 000 said the same thing.

It is also interesting to note that 55 per cent of older householders claim they throw away no fresh food, compared with only 13 per cent of young singles and 6 per cent of young parents. This could mean either that as people become older they waste less or that people who are now old grew up in a thriftier era and have maintained that attitude. Undoubtedly, attitudes to consuming have changed greatly in recent decades, suggesting that young wasters today will turn into old wasters tomorrow.

FIGURE 9: Average spending on wasted fresh food, by
household income, 2004

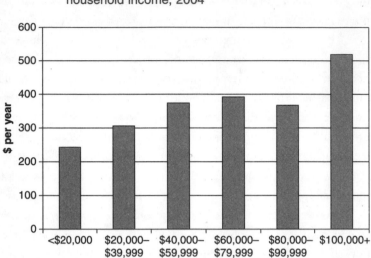

Guilt or indifference?

The survey results suggest that Australia is a wasteful society, yet there are good reasons for thinking that the amount of waste reported is much less than is actually the case. Some important items were omitted from the survey, such as the money we spend on toys, cars and, perhaps the biggest item, houses that have more space than we can reasonably use. There is also reason to think that the survey respondents were reluctant to admit the full extent of their wasteful spending. We know, for example, that the average household could cut its electricity bill by 10–15 per cent by adopting a few simple measures,[7] such as turning lights off, having shorter showers and not leaving the television in stand-by mode, yet the survey results show that we think we could cut our bills by only 7.5 per cent. Households admit to throwing out $4.6 billion of fresh food each year (and waste an additional $0.6 billion on unfinished drinks), yet audits of household garbage bins suggest that the true figure is closer to $8 billion.[8]

The survey results also provide some insights into how we feel about our wasteful spending. The practice of buying things we do not use is widespread in Australia, even though most Australians feel guilty about it. When asked to rank themselves on a scale from one to five in response to the statements 'When I buy items that don't get used I feel guilty' and 'When I buy items that don't get used it doesn't bother me', 61 per cent of respondents reported some level of guilt and, of those, 40 per cent reported high levels of guilt. Perhaps not surprisingly, people who admit to wasting more also claim to feel less guilty about it. Among those who waste less than $10 a fortnight on food, 69 per cent feel guilty about buying things that don't get used, whereas only 44 per cent of householders who waste more than $50 say they feel guilty.

For a decade now, governments, schools and the media have emphasised the 'reduce, re-use, recycle' message: we could expect young people to be more aware of the environmental damage caused by waste and take a stronger stand against it. But this might not be the case. Although 47 per cent of older householders say they feel very guilty about buying items that do not get used, only 29 per cent of those in young single households feel the same way, although the concern rises to 44 per cent among young couples and to 41 per cent among young parents. And, even though they have much higher levels of wasteful consumption, richer households feel less guilty about spending money on things that don't get used than less wealthy households (see Figure 10).

FIGURE 10: Proportion strongly agreeing with the statement
'When I buy items that don't get used I feel guilty',
by household income

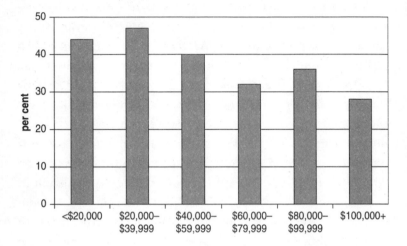

Despite the survey revealing high levels of wasteful consumption, Australians see themselves as cautious shoppers who rarely buy anything they don't need: 80 per cent claim that they think carefully about how much use they are going to get out of the things they buy, and 72 per cent say they hardly ever buy things that don't get used. It seems that we feel guilty when we buy things we don't use and at the same time claim that we don't buy such things. But the facts show that we spend huge sums on all sorts of goods that go unused. This suggests that Australians live in a state of denial about the amount of money they waste on things they don't need and lends support to the argument that much of the pleasure gained from shopping comes from the act of buying rather than from using the goods bought. If we really did think carefully about how much use we would get from a purchase, retailers would not put so much effort into creating the conditions for impulse buying. Few of us are willing to admit that we are manipulated into buying something on impulse: instead, we tell ourselves we had been looking for just such a product for a while or we hadn't noticed that gadget before but now we'd like to have one.

Most people believe advertising works but that they themselves are immune to it. Similarly, we deny that we personally are prone to buying things we never use, yet we are quick to point the finger at others. Eighty per cent of survey respondents agreed with the statement 'Most Australians buy and consume far more than they need: it's wasteful'. This means four in five Australians believe themselves to be careful shoppers who rarely buy unnecessary things but acknowledge that Australian society is characterised by high levels of aimless spending.

We need a reality check if we are to reduce the mountains of waste we generate each year.

The effluent society

Australians are among the greatest generators of landfill in the world. US and Israeli citizens come equal first, with an impressive 730 kilograms of waste per person in 2001, and Australians come a respectable fourth, with 690 kilograms.[9] Some rich countries are much less wasteful: New Zealanders, for example, created 400 kilograms of waste per person, while Canadians confined it to only 350, less than half that of their cousins across the 49th parallel.

Waste is inseparable from the spread of affluenza. Marketers work hard to create the idea that the goods they are selling are desirable even though they know that, once they have succeeded and a sale has been made, work must immediately begin on the process of selling a replacement. Buying brands, not wearing them, increases profits. Changes in fashion and our restless wish to renew ourselves through buying things—as opposed to changes in our needs—lead to billions of dollars spent on clothes, shoes, furnishings, electrical appliances, cars, toys, and so on, and on. Changes in fashion create billions of dollars of waste as goods are either thrown away or put into storage long before they need to be replaced. Our bigger wardrobes, attics and self-storage units act as halfway houses for stuff that we are not yet ready to admit is redundant and is money wasted. We put things back in the fridge, telling ourselves we might use them up but really knowing we need another week to get over the guilt of discarding now.

Fashion is not, of course, the only way for marketers to increase our spending and disposing. Obsolescence is a feature of the consumer electronics industry. The transformation of music collections from vinyl to CDs took a couple of decades, but the switch from CDs to MP3 players is taking just a few years. No doubt, consumers are preparing themselves for the day when MP4 makes their MP3 players and the music stored on them as useful as a cassette player or home movie projector. Some consumers will not even have to wait for MP4 to come along: the rechargeable battery on the Apple iPod cannot be replaced when it wears out. But our attitudes are as important as marketing in creating a disposable society. Slowly but surely, during the past few decades most Australians have moved from asking themselves 'Do I really need a new one?' to 'Why should I make do with the current one?'

Another strategy the marketers use involves exploiting our love of 'a bargain'. Receiving much more product for a slightly higher price strikes us as good value. The fact that we have wasted our money by buying more than we need is often overlooked in our haste to 'get our money's worth'. This trend is most apparent in the fast food industry, where we can double the amount of calories for an extra dollar, but it is pervasive. How many times have you rented three videos when you thought you wanted only one? It seems like great value to get two more for an extra $2, but if you don't actually have time to watch them it is just a waste of money.

When it comes to the problem of how to deal with the piles of waste we produce, the focus is typically on where to bury it—not where it came from. The long-term solution to mountains of waste is not more landfill sites but fewer shopping centres. In the world's rich countries, government agencies with the task of reducing the amount of waste going to landfill are facing a crisis. Recycling did offset the growth in waste for a few years, but we seem to be reaching the limits of our willingness to recycle, and consumer demand is now overwhelming our concern for the environment.

The 'reduce, re-use, recycle' mantra has been widely adopted, yet all the effort has gone into the 'recycling' and 're-use' messages and none into the reduce message. Reducing consumption is bad for retailers, of course. And it can even be argued that the availability of recycling bins makes it easier for some people to rationalise their decision to consume wastefully. Each year in Australia nearly 20 million tonnes of waste goes to landfill.[10] In 1992 all Australian governments agreed to aim to reduce by 50 per cent the amount of waste going to landfill. There has been progress, but twelve years on we are nowhere near reaching the 50 per cent target.[11]

The news is going to get worse. As discussed, rich households waste more than households with moderate incomes. More worryingly, wealthy people are less likely to feel guilty about spending wastefully and much more likely to qualify as 'who cares?' wasters. While 47 per cent of respondents from households earning between $20 000 and $39 999 said they feel guilty when they buy something they don't use, only 27 per cent of respondents from households earning over $100 000 feel that way. Many Australians are now simply too wealthy to care or too busy to bother thinking about the goods and services they really need. Average incomes will probably double in the next 35 years, and this bodes ill for Australia's environment. As we grow richer we are more prone to waste. The trend towards recycling has slowed the volume of waste, but it cannot halt its inexorable accumulation.

Of course, Australians are not alone in wasting billions of dollars on goods they don't use and services they don't need. A US study found that Americans threw away an estimated US$43 billion of food in 2001.[12] Up to one-fifth of the United States' food goes to waste, the average citizen sending 59 kilograms of food to landfill each year. A study of wasteful consumption in the United Kingdom found that Britons discard £80.6 billion of unused goods and services each year—enough to cover government spending on transport, defence, industry, agriculture, employment and housing.[13]

Disposal of waste is seen as a growing environmental problem around the world, but it is the creation of waste that makes the modern market economy go round. We cannot solve the waste problem without solving the consumption problem.

Chapter 8
Spending ourselves sick

You do look glum! What you need is a gramme of soma.

——Aldous Huxley, *Brave New World*

The drugged culture

This book arose out of one observation. Despite the huge improvements in our material wellbeing in the last 50 years, we have become no happier. It can even be argued that we are less happy than we were when our incomes were only a third of what they are now. Yet, with the exception of Indigenous Australians—who seem to be experiencing all the sicknesses of affluence but few of the benefits—Australians have never been physically healthier. Despite this, we are more obsessed with and anxious about our health, which is both a sign of social malaise and a golden marketing opportunity.

Perhaps the best indication of how we are travelling as a nation is provided by measures of our psychological health. The proliferation of the diseases of affluence suggests that the psychological wellbeing of people in rich countries is in decline. Among these illnesses are drug dependence, obesity, loneliness, and a suite of psychological disorders ranging from depression, anxiety and compulsive behaviours to widespread but ill-defined anomie. Possibly the most telling evidence is the very high prevalence of depression in rich countries:

- In the five decades after World War II—the golden age of economic growth—the incidence of depression in the United States increased tenfold.[1]
- The top ten diseases affecting young men in Australia are all psychological disorders or forms of substance abuse.
- In France nearly one in four people is taking tranquillisers, antidepressants, antipsychotics or other mood-altering drugs[2]— a proportion similar to that in the United States.
- One in six British adults (17.2 per cent) suffers from mental health problems, with anxiety–depressive disorders accounting for more than half of these.[3]
- The World Health Organization and the World Bank say that major depression—already the biggest cause of disability—is expected to become the world's second most burdensome disease by 2020.[4]

No wonder antidepressant drugs that have no side-effects are now the Holy Grail of pharmaceutical corporations.

Modern Australians appear so beset by anxiety, depression and alienation that they consume enormous quantities of drugs and other substances to help them make it through the day.[5] The 2002 National Health Survey found that at any one time 13 per cent of Australian adults admit they experience high or very high levels of psychological distress, while an additional 23 per cent report moderate levels.[6] High levels of distress are often episodic, so the figures would be substantially higher if taken over a year. The survey also revealed an astonishing but unremarked fact: 18 per cent of Australian adults reported that in the two weeks preceding the survey they had used medication to improve their mental wellbeing.[7] In the main, the medications were sleeping tablets (4.1 per cent), antidepressants (4.7 per cent), vitamin and mineral supplements such as vitamin B for stress (7.8 per cent) and natural medications such as St John's Wort for anxiety and depression (5.4 per cent). Again, many people go on and off various forms of medication, so we would expect that over a year the proportion of Australians taking drugs for their mental wellbeing would be considerably higher than 18 per cent.

Prescribed and natural medicines are not the only substances Australians take in the hope of dealing with psychological distress. Alcohol and illicit drugs can also serve as psychological props. For males, 'risky' use of alcohol is defined as consumption of 29 or more standard drinks a week (more than four a day); for females, the figure is fifteen or more standard drinks a week (more than two a day).[8] When we add together high-risk alcohol use and medications taken for mental wellbeing, we find that 27 per cent of Australians aged more than eighteen years rely on mood-altering substances to cope with daily life.

There are gender differences in patterns of substance use (see Figure 11). In general, men are more likely to seek refuge in alcohol, although risky alcohol use declines among men aged more than 55 years; women are more likely to turn to pills. When the numbers are broken down by age group, it is apparent that young people are less likely to resort to legal substances to deal with the vicissitudes of life: 23 per cent of 18- to 34-year-olds do so, compared with 28 per cent for older Australians (see

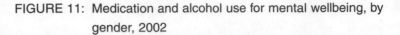

FIGURE 11: Medication and alcohol use for mental wellbeing, by gender, 2002

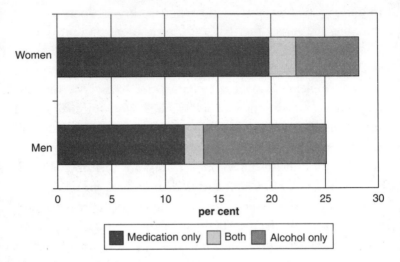

Figure 12). This calls into question the notion that old age ushers in a period of psychological calm. Although total use of medications and alcohol varies little by income group, low-income people are much more likely to rely on medications and higher income people are more likely to rely on alcohol.

These figures take no account of the third major response to mental distress—illicit drugs. Most people who take illicit drugs do so only occasionally and recreationally, but some depend on them as a means of coping with life. This is most apparent in the case of addictive drugs (notably heroin) but it also applies to people who cannot get by without using marijuana daily. In recent years illicit drugs appear to be replacing alcohol as a major social risk: a third of the drivers killed on Victorian roads tested positive to illicit drugs (especially opiates and amphetamines); this is a higher proportion

FIGURE 12: Medication and alcohol use for mental wellbeing, by age, 2002

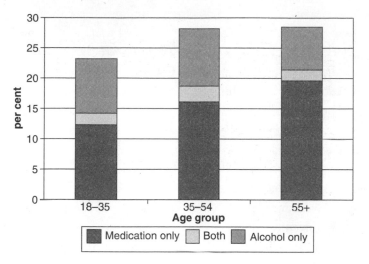

than those with alcohol in their blood.[9] Most experts say more than half of prison inmates are incarcerated for crimes linked to drugs.

The data do not allow us to separate out 'therapeutic' from recreational use of illicit drugs. Nor do they allow us to distinguish between people who use illicit drugs only and people who use illicit drugs in combination with alcohol or medications such as antidepressants. We do know, however, that illicit drug use is very widespread in Australia: in 2002 the Australian Institute of Health and Welfare found that 17 per cent of people aged more than fourteen years had used illicit drugs in the preceding twelve months (20 per cent for males and 14 per cent for females) and nearly two in five people had used them at some time in their life.[10] Young people's lower reliance on medications and alcohol is offset by their heavier use of illicit drugs. If we were to aggregate medications, alcohol and illicit drugs being used for mental well-being, it is likely that at least 30 per cent of Australian adults rely on drugs and substances to get them through the day. Why is there so much distress in an affluent, secure society such as ours?

Social problems are often turned into private travails by being medicalised. The increase in prescription of Ritalin to control attention deficit hyperactivity disorder, especially among teenage boys, is a good illustration of the phenomenon. Another is the increased use of medication and surgical procedures to deal with obesity: medicalisation of the problem not only provides work for doctors and markets for drug companies, it also allows us to avoid conceding that perhaps we have created an 'obesogenic' environment, that is, a social environment that promotes and facilitates obesity.

It is convenient for the consumer society to interpret and deal with social pathologies as personal disorders. After all, we are meant to be happy. Economists and politicians have long been promising that greater material wealth will create a better society. Like all rich countries, Australia is obsessed with economic growth and higher incomes. But if, after accounting for changes in the cost of living, we are three times richer than Australians were in the 1950s, why is our society characterised by an epidemic of mental disorders and high levels of substance abuse? High-income earners are just as dependent as low-income earners.

The fact that close to a third of adult Australians depend on drugs or other substances to get them through the day stands in contrast to our imagined identity as a nation of carefree people who take life in their stride. It clashes, too, with the marketers' images of customers who have found bliss by using this brand of shampoo or driving that brand of car. For decades we have all been striving for the good life. Now that it is within reach for most of us, a large proportion of the population seems to need medications and other substances to avoid falling into a more or less permanent state of anxiety, depression and despair—a state that might be a more accurate reflection of the emptiness of modern consumerism than the happy faces the advertisers show us. Psychologists are aware of the link between affluenza and psychological disorders:

> Existing scientific research on the value of materialism yields clear and consistent findings. People who are highly focused on materialistic values have lower personal wellbeing and psychological health than those who believe that materialistic pursuits are relatively unimportant.[11]

When our political leaders talk of 'families doing it tough' and 'struggling Australians' they can't be talking about material deprivation. Without dismissing the genuine hardship experienced by the 10 to 20 per cent at the bottom of the income distribution, after decades of economic growth most Australians are doing very well. Subliminally, the rhetoric of struggle might be appealing to the psychological distress that seems to be so widespread and deep-rooted in this rich land of ours. It is hard to avoid the conclusion that the epidemic of psychological disorders is, at least in part, the price we are paying for decades of economic reform, the ceaseless promotion of market values, and the associated erosion of traditional supports in family and community.

Making money from misery

A society that is feeling anxious, depressed, dissatisfied and inadequate provides fertile ground for the sellers of things that promise to make us happy. And the beauty of it is that when we feel like that we are more likely to want to spend money anyway, which makes us particularly vulnerable to the marketers' ruses. Drug companies engage in disease-mongering by describing, medicalising and exaggerating normal problems and turning them into clinical conditions. Even when it is not necessary to manufacture a disease or disorder because it is already widespread, the medical industry intervenes in a way that transforms social maladies into personal problems. We then come to believe that there is something wrong with *us*, rather than something wrong with society. This protects the social order from radical criticism. The medical industry serves to calm the eruptions of social distress by diverting blame from social structures to 'dysfunctional' individuals.

Few groups in society are more vulnerable to promises than the sick and the dying. So it should not come as a surprise to learn that, as a group, pharmaceutical companies are among the largest contributors to the worldwide advertising industry. In 2004 one of Australia's most popular women's magazines, *Woman's Day*, ran advertisements for meningococcal vaccinations, depicting the feet of a corpse with a mortuary label tied to a toe. The label peeled off the page, and readers were urged, 'Take this to your GP and ask about vaccination today'. The information on the mortuary tag said that adults account for nearly half of all cases of disease caused by the C-strain of the meningococcus bacterium and that, among infected adults, two in ten lose digits or limbs and one in ten dies. The advertisement failed to say that the disease affects only about 130 adults in Australia each year and that most make a full recovery. The campaign was billed as 'a community message from Baxter Healthcare'. At the same time, separate ads running in the specialist medical press advised doctors that 'patients may be bringing in coupons requesting vaccinations'. Australian law prevents pharmaceutical companies from advertising prescription drugs directly to consumers, so the companies are increasingly conducting 'community education campaigns'.

Supporters of the selective use of statistics to frighten people into asking their doctors for unnecessary treatments see this as effective marketing. Consumerism creates the problem and then offers a cure. Drug companies respond to affluent societies' growing neuroticism about health by developing strategies for creating new markets for drugs where the demand is underdeveloped or trailing off. This is known in the trade as 'disease-mongering', defined as 'widening the boundaries of treatable illness in order to expand markets for those who sell and deliver treatments'.[12] It is achieved by exaggerating, legitimising and medicalising our anxieties and inadequacies.

One of the more blatant attempts at disease-mongering was promoted by two major pharmaceutical companies that were salivating at the massive profits Pfizer was earning from its anti-impotence drug Viagra. If men suffered from a disorder that impaired their sex life, perhaps a similar problem could be found in women, so they set about defining 'female sexual dysfunction' and turning it into a recognised medical condition treatable with drugs. The companies convened a series of conferences and meetings, involving university researchers and colleagues in the pharmaceutical industry, so as to define a new illness that doctors would see as needing medical intervention. Noting that the release of Viagra had earned Pfizer $1.5 billion in 2001, Bayer and Lilly hoped to make comparable amounts from women anxious about their sexual performance. Ray Moynihan, the Australian medical journalist who exposed the plan, wrote:

To build similar markets for drugs among women, companies first require a clearly defined medical diagnosis with measurable characteristics to facilitate credible clinical trial. Over the past six years the pharmaceutical industry has funded, and its representatives have in some cases attended, a series of meetings to come up with just such a definition.[13]

A vital component of the campaign to define the new disorder was an article published in 1999 that claimed 43 per cent of women aged 18 to 59 experience female sexual dysfunction, or FSD. Only later did it become known that two of the three authors had links to Pfizer and that the 43 per cent figure included a large number of women who had answered 'yes' when asked in a survey whether they had experienced any of seven problems for two months or more during the preceding year, including a lack of desire for sex and anxiety about sexual performance. Critics pointed out that loss of libido is quite normal when women are faced with stress, fatigue or relationship difficulties. Yet the figure was widely quoted in the media, thereby creating the general impression, especially among doctors, that female sexual dysfunction is a widespread disorder that requires treatment—preferably with one of the drugs being developed by pharmaceutical companies. If we consider that among the causes of lack of desire for sex are exhaustion from overwork and tensions arising from overconsumption, it is apparent that once again the market has responded with a solution to a problem of its own making.

When the leading advocate of the existence of the disorder, a professor of urology and gynaecology at Boston University, was asked 'whether marketing campaigns worth hundreds of millions of dollars may ultimately tend to amplify particular views of sexual difficulties and promote certain therapeutic options over others, he said: "I'm an academic clinical doctor. That's a question for some philosopher"".[14] The medical researchers colluding in the manufacturing of disease might want to avoid the ethical pitfalls, but there is little doubt that the marketers of any drug to cure female sexual dysfunction would recognise that the primary market would not be women anxious about their sexual performance but men who feel they are sexually deprived and see the problem as being the fault of their partners.

The process by which female sexual dysfunction was created as a clinical condition is typical of disease-mongering.[15] The manufacturing of a new disease, often camouflaged as a public awareness campaign, is often the result of an informal alliance of researchers, drug companies and consumer groups, all of whom have an interest in raising the profile of the disorder in question. The media find medical stories irresistible and willingly collaborate in the propagation of worrying information about the prevalence of a previously unrecognised disease. Medicalisation of normal conditions trades on our fears about health and can contribute to cost blow-outs in the public health system as patients demand treatment. Ray Moynihan and colleagues add, 'At a deeper level it may help to feed unhealthy obsessions with health, obscure or mystify sociological or political explanations for health problems, and focus undue attention on pharmacological, individualised, or privatised solutions'.[16]

The researchers who exposed disease-mongering in the *British Medical Journal* also gave as examples the pharmaceutical industry's approach to baldness, osteoporosis, erectile dysfunction and irritable bowel syndrome. The last-mentioned condition is, for most people who suffer from it, a mild functional disorder requiring no more than reassurance, yet it 'is currently being reframed as a serious disease attracting a label and a drug, with all the associated harms and costs'. Secret documents from a PR company working for GlaxoSmithKline set out an 'education programme' designed to see irritable bowel syndrome 'established in the minds of doctors as a significant and discrete disease state'. The company devised a plan to create a market for Glaxo's drug Lotronex by targeting promotional material at doctors, nurses, pharmacists and patients.

SAD

Soon after the terrorist attacks on the World Trade Center, full-page advertisements appearing in the *New York Times* stated, 'Millions suffer from chronic anxiety . . . millions could be helped by Paxil'. The text of the advertisements listed the symptoms of anxiety as fatigue, worry, restlessness and muscle tension. Apart from the fact that such symptoms could describe almost anybody or any illness, it should scarcely be surprising that people would feel anxious living in New York soon after September 11.[17] The city's residents were being conditioned to ask for Paxil whenever they felt anxious: given the levels of anxiety likely to be experienced by New Yorkers during the 'war on terror', such an association in only a small proportion of the population is likely to be a profitable one. The television news serves as a daily advertisement for Paxil.

The re-labelling of human emotions as 'disorders', together with the subsequent prescription of medication to treat them, is increasingly common. People who would have once described themselves as shy might now describe themselves as suffering from social anxiety disorder, or SAD, also known as social phobia. According to information produced by support groups, among the most common situations to be feared by SAD sufferers are speaking in public, eating and drinking in public, meeting new people, being the centre of attention, meeting or talking with people in positions of authority, meeting or talking to members of the opposite sex, being teased, and being criticised. The main symptoms are as follows:

- high levels of anxiety when exposed to the feared situation—palpitations, trembling, sweating, tense muscles, dry throat, blushing, dizziness, a sinking feeling in the stomach
- an overwhelming feeling of wanting to escape
- feelings of self-consciousness and inadequacy
- avoidance of the feared situation—which can often lead to isolation from friends, family and society
- reliance on drugs or alcohol to get the person through the feared situation.

It is said that SAD usually develops in the mid-teenage years. Although some people's lives are dominated by their inability to participate easily in social settings, it is entirely normal for adolescents to experience feelings of self-consciousness and inadequacy and so try to avoid situations that are likely to make them feel anxious. As noted in Chapter 3, it is precisely these teenager characteristics the tobacco companies set out to exploit. Portraying the feelings and anxieties of normal emotional development as 'symptoms' of a disorder that can then be treated by a drug is a form of disease-mongering.

In this case the drug company behind the disease-mongering was Roche, which wanted to create a market for its anti-depressant Aurorix. In 1997 Roche's PR company issued a media release claiming that more than one million Australians suffer from the psychiatric disorder known as social phobia.[18] Roche backed a patient group called the Obsessive Compulsive and Anxiety Disorders Foundation of Victoria and lined up 'independent' medical experts to claim that social phobia is a widespread but under-diagnosed medical condition. A pharmaceutical marketing guide used the campaign as an example to be emulated, noting, 'Social phobia was recognised in the US and so transatlantic opinion leaders were mobilised to participate in advisory activities, meetings, publications, etc. to help influence the overall belief in Europe'.[19]

Surely a doctor who swears 'I will prevent disease whenever I can, for prevention is preferable to cure' would never go along with these drug company rackets. Most people believe that advertising works, but that they themselves are immune. Doctors pride themselves on their capacity to make clinical decisions based on all the evidence and insist that they are not influenced by marketing. If this is true, the pharmaceutical companies are wasting billions on marketing aimed at doctors, with everything from logo-embossed prescription pads to conferences and seminars on tropical islands. According to one study:

> A randomly selected group of practicing doctors said that scientific sources are much more important in influencing their prescribing than are commercial sources. However, when questioned about the usefulness of two classes of drugs where the message from the scientific literature was opposite that in

the commercial literature the majority of doctors in this group held commercial beliefs about these two classes. Therefore, it appears that physicians can be influenced by promotional literature without being aware of it.[20]

Medicalisation of the human condition has been described as a 'process by which non-medical problems become defined and treated as medical problems, usually in terms of illnesses and disorders'.[21] The process of medicalisation turns attention away from the social environment to the behaviour and flaws of individuals. The market will come up with a solution for every human problem, and the process of disease-mongering reinforces the belief that happiness is just another purchase away.

The ideal body

The values of the market are transforming our physical bodies as well as our minds. Huge industries are devoted to changing our shapes, our faces and our life spans, all in pursuit of the notion of happiness purveyed by the market. Cosmetic surgery is one form of 'luxury consumption' that is booming. In Australia in 1999 about 300 000 cosmetic procedures were performed (including chemical peels, collagen injections and laser skin resurfacing), representing an increase of 50 per cent from 1995.[22] Customers are increasingly young people who are seeking to 'normalise' themselves by having 'defects' surgically eliminated.

A cosmetic procedure is now commonly given as a Christmas or twenty-first birthday present. Breast implants are the most popular gift, followed by liposuction and facial surgery. Nearly all cases involve men buying cosmetic surgery for their wives or partners.[23] A breast augmentation costs $7000, and the gift voucher comes with a swimsuit in the desired cup size so that the 'husband has something other than the gift voucher to put under the tree'.[24] The gift package for a facelift costs around $10 000 but includes a range of make-up products so that the recipient can look her best after the operation—or perhaps cover up the bruising and scars. Mothers tend to give their daughters nose jobs; men tend to give their partners facelifts or liposuction. Dads give their sons orthodontic treatments and young men give their girl-friends breast implants.[25] Instances of women giving their boyfriends or husbands gift vouchers for penile enlargement appear to be rare.

In the United States, in what is described as 'the latest vanity craze sweeping the nation', Botox parties provide a congenial envi-ronment in which guests drink champagne and take it in turns to have injections to paralyse their facial muscles. The product is described as 'the wrinkle-free fountain of youth'. But this is trivial compared with the plot of the television program *Extreme Makeover*. Thousands apply to win the chance to have their appearance transformed. Millions watch, and the renovation is carried out by an 'extreme team' of plastic surgeons, dentists, personal trainers, and hair, make-up and wardrobe stylists. One of the early winners, Melissa, had a nose job, breast implants, brow lift, tummy tuck, ears pinned and Lasik surgery. She had her teeth whitened and straightened too. Another winner, David, a 38-year-old member of the National Guard, who believed his appearance had barred him from promotion, received a nose job, chin aug-mentation, neck lift, brow lift, upper and lower eye lifts, tooth whitening and porcelain veneers.[26]

The viewers thought, 'Wow, why not?' The answer, of course, is that these extreme measures can fail or have tragic consequences. An Australian study found that women who have had cosmetic surgery are more likely to have chronic illnesses and to resort to medication for anxiety and sleep disorders.[27] A Swedish study found that women with breast implants are three times more likely than members of the general population to commit suicide.[28] It is not clear whether psychological disorders lead people to cosmetic surgery or whether cosmetic surgery induces psychological disorders, although the Swedish researchers refer to 'the well-documented link between psychiatric disorders and a desire for cosmetic surgery'. Cosmetic surgeons are sometimes described as psychiatrists with knives.

The boom in cosmetic surgery exemplifies the growing divergence in modern consumer society between the actual self and the ideal self. It also illustrates how the ideal self has become increasingly externalised, as an image of the body. There are, of course, genuine instances where plastic surgery is warranted, but apart from that the desire for perfection—engendered by the media, with their distorted images of the bodily ideal—builds the market for cosmetic surgery. The traditional role of doctors is to consider the patient's symptoms, make a diagnosis and recommend a treatment, but in the case of most cosmetic surgery the media manufacture the symptoms and make the diagnosis and the 'patient' then tells the doctor what the treatment should be.

Part Three

What can we do?

Chapter 9
The politics of affluenza

Almost never before in the history of the world has there been a happier country than contemporary Australia.

———Health Minister Tony Abbott, December 2004

The myth of the Aussie battler

Politicians love to identify with the Aussie battler, that stoic, resilient character who has little and complains less. Fifty years ago Australia was full of battlers, people hardened by the rigours of depression and war and, if not proud of their penury, certainly not ashamed of it. The Aussie battler is the central icon of Australian political folklore, and the image persists despite the fact that, as a result of sustained economic growth in the past five decades, the number of people who truly struggle has shrunk to a small proportion of the population. Yet, as Chapter 4 points out, for every genuine battler there are three or four who imagine they fit the description. That is why our political leaders keep the myth of the battler alive and exploit it for all it's worth.

Hansard, the verbatim record of the Federal Parliament, shows that in the eighteen months from January 2003 to August 2004 politicians referred to 'battlers' 237 times, 'struggling families'

54 times and Australians 'doing it tough' 65 times. This could simply reflect the politicians' propensity to speak in cliches, but their choice of cliches is revealing. One senior minister even referred to battlers who earn more than $60 000 a year. Another referred to the tax cuts of the 2003 budget—which went over-whelmingly to high-income earners—as rewarding the battlers.

The place of the Aussie battler in the national psyche is rein-forced by the media. A Commonwealth Bank survey of savings behaviour in 2002 concluded that 60 per cent of Australians were finding it hard to cover their living expenses, a big increase on the previous year's 48 per cent. The bank described these people as 'struggling'. Media reports interpreted the survey results as sup-porting the belief that the bulk of the population were finding it difficult to make ends meet. In Canberra, one of the wealthiest areas of Australia (and the world), the local newspaper led with 'Almost half of all Canberra households are struggling to cover their living expenses, let alone save for a rainy day, new research has shown'.[1] The article went on to discuss the position of the lowest income groups who depend on charity, as if the circum-stances of people living in poverty are equivalent to those of middle-class mortgagees: 'The figures have alarmed local welfare and charity groups, who believe the trends could push more resi-dents into financial crisis'.

A similar message was delivered by a series of prominent stories in a Sydney newspaper. Under the headline 'Families sucked into mortgage nightmare', the paper reported on a 'crisis in housing affordability', with one in five households in 'mortgage stress'.[2] The tenor of the articles was that large numbers of Sydney resi-dents found themselves under financial pressure because of the size of their mortgage repayments compared with their incomes.

Expressions such as 'people with mortgages are hurting', 'crisis looms', 'problems have undoubtedly become more severe' and 'real hardship areas' serve to reinforce the popular impression that most Australians are doing it tough and are trapped in a difficult situation that is not of their making.

Yet the 'mortgage stress' that generated the headlines is not the unexpected result of rising interest rates or falling incomes: it is the result of luxury fever, which has driven thousands of individuals to borrow more money than they can comfortably repay in order to satisfy their escalating acquisitiveness. In other words, many people have set their sights on levels of comfort and luxury they cannot afford and have taken on too much debt in order to get there. The newspaper reports make little distinction between, on one hand, poor households in genuine difficulty because they cannot afford rising rents even in poorer suburbs and, on the other, wealthy households in mortgage stress as a result of $500 000 mortgages on large houses in wealthy suburbs. The press coverage also notes that apartment buyers in Sydney's CBD and nearby suburbs are most affected by mortgage stress. One couple with monthly repayments of more than $2000 bemoaned their decision to delay having a baby because 'they had their hearts set on buying a home in Baulkham Hills', a reasonably expensive outer suburb. The male of the pair was quoted as saying, '. . . this is what I have to pay to maintain this lifestyle. I could go and live in Tasmania if I wanted. But I don't want to. I want to live here'.

In earlier times, when wealthy people made decisions to live beyond their means, their financial difficulties attracted little public sympathy. If they complained it would perhaps be suggested that they might live a little less grandly. Today, though, newspapers, commentators and political leaders speak as though the imagined financial difficulties of the wealthy are the result of hard times rather than inflated expectations. The problem then becomes a matter of public concern. The real concerns of yesterday's poor have become the imagined concerns of today's rich. Struggle Street, it seems, has become crowded; the trouble is the new residents want to build McMansions there.

One effect of this conflation of the poorest citizens' circumstances with those of the wealthy majority is to reinforce a widespread belief that times are difficult—despite the fact that we are richer than we have ever been and much richer than the vast majority of people in the world. Deprivation syndrome persuades politicians to distort policy to 'reduce the burden of taxation' and to increase welfare payments to middle-class households that are living lives that would, in other places and at other times, be regarded as luxurious. This emphasis on the tribulations of the middle class not only validates the self-centred preoccupation of wealthy people with their own financial circumstances: it crowds out sympathy for those who are genuinely struggling. And it helps to explain why, after decades of sustained economic growth that have seen average incomes increase several times, the Aussie battler has not disappeared from public discourse but has instead become more prevalent than ever. It is hard to avoid the conclusion that political parties have deliberately fomented dissatisfaction among the middle class in order to perpetuate the myth of the Aussie battler, for they can then claim to understand their pain and offer solutions. The little Aussie battler has turned into the great Australian whinger.

Nowhere was this better illustrated than in the 2004 federal election, won resoundingly by the Liberal–National Party Coalition. It wasn't the extraordinary public spending spree of the conservative government during the election campaign that sank the Labor Party: it was the private consumption binge of the previous decade. Booming house prices coupled with an unprecedented level of consumer debt have left most Australians absorbed by their own material circumstances, with little room left for thoughts of building a better society. Motivated not by financial need but by the very aspirations Labor leader Mark Latham lauded, Australian households found themselves in debt up to their necks, and that meant that during the campaign hundreds of thousands of people looked at their partners across the kitchen table and said, 'If interest rates go up by a couple of per cent we're stuffed'.

Having the bank foreclose on you must be a nasty experience, especially if you have measured your success and place in society by the pile of things you possess. During the 2004 election campaign many economists pointed out that interest rates were no more likely to rise under a Labor government than under a Coalition one, but if nothing other than money really matters to a voter why take the risk of voting Labor?

This is where we have got to after twenty years of creeping affluenza—an era in which materialism and its attendant self-absorption have invaded the consciousness of most Australians. The Coalition victory reflected nothing more than the pre-occupation with self that characterises modern Australia after two decades of market ideology and sustained growth. It was particularly disquieting to witness the disengagement of large numbers of young people who seemed barely aware an election was on. Education systems' increasing emphasis on vocational training at the expense of understanding self and society, coupled with the narcissism of the consumer culture in which these young people have grown up, mean that, while despair for the future of democracy is warranted, we should expect nothing more.

Breaking with the pattern of the previous few elections of relying on spin rather than real policy differences to tempt voters, during the 2004 election campaign the Labor Party did actually issue some policies that differentiated it from the conservatives—policies aimed at creating a fairer society and taking away some of the more unjustifiable forms of middle-class welfare typical of the Howard years. Labor's promise to redirect Commonwealth funding from the wealthiest private schools to poorer ones is the best example. But even this was a victim of Labor's schizoid campaign, in which it tried to embrace both the self-centred individualism of neoliberalism and the appeal to fairness of social democracy, a contradiction embodied in the Party's leader. In the dreams of aspirational voters, Mark Latham's 'ladder of opportunity' leads to Geelong Grammar or The King's School. For many, taking money from such elite schools is akin to removing the top rungs of Mr Latham's ladder.

Of course, relentless promotion of self-interest and rejection of the politics of social progress are no more than we should expect of the Liberal Party. It is, after all, the essence of liberalism. Liberals have always maintained that asserting individual freedoms, not building a better society, is the object of politics. Nevertheless, one of the founders of liberalism, John Stuart Mill, could see the danger of ending up where we are today. In 1865 he wrote that he was not persuaded that 'trampling, crushing, elbowing, and treading on each other's heels . . . are the most desirable lot of humankind'.[3] These qualities of the aspirational society he saw as the 'disagreeable symptoms of one of the phases of industrial progress'—regrettably, a phase that has been much more enduring than Mill could have imagined.

Australian politicians of both persuasions talk ad nauseam of 'struggling families' and devise policies that pander to the imagined woes of the middle class. As long as we remain preoccupied with house prices, credit card debts, interest rates, tax cuts and getting ahead financially—in other words, as long as we define our success in life through money—Labor can expect to win an election only by mimicking the Liberal Party.

Middle-class welfare

One of the consequences of the imagined hardship of the middle class, and the enduring myth of the Aussie battler, is that the Federal Government has felt the need to provide billions of dollars in welfare payments to households that have no need of them. The politics of self-interest has cultivated a widespread sense of entitlement, a perception that the government owes people something after taxing their hard-earned income. Government offers various rationales for these hand-outs: the payments act as incentives for self-provision of various services; the recipients deserve it because having children is expensive; it's a reward for working hard.

This is a strange inversion of the arguments about welfare for the poor. The problem with giving poor people welfare, we are told, is that hand-outs discourage them from providing for themselves. They become less self-reliant and more dependent on charity. It also reduces the efficiency of the economy because higher tax rates are needed to fund generous welfare payments. This view of welfare payments is common in Australian political debate, and not just from the conservative side of politics. Its popularity masks the hypocrisy on which it is often based. We are told that welfare payments for wealthy people act as *incentives* to take more responsibility for their own health care and retirement incomes and to have more children, while welfare payments to poor people act as *disincentives* to work and to take responsibility for themselves. It is not clear why middle-class recipients of welfare are deemed immune from its harmful effects. Support for poor single mothers is derided; support for wealthy mothers, in the form of the non–means tested family payments, just helps them meet the cost of having children.

Welfare payments and tax concessions to Australia's middle class and the wealthy have become rife:

- The 30 per cent rebate for private health insurance costs $2.5 billion a year. Half of this goes to the richest third of Australian taxpayers.
- Family Tax Benefit Part B, which was designed to help families with the expense of raising children, costs more than $400 million a year. It is not means tested, so a large proportion of it goes to families who experience no hardship.
- The Federal Government pays parents $3000 (rising to $5000 in 2008) for each new baby. This will cost $3.5 billion over four years. No one asks why low-income taxpayers should fund a windfall for wealthy people who decide to have a baby.
- The First Home Owners grant of $7000 was not means tested and many high-income people who were about to buy houses received a windfall. Some wealthy parents bought their children apartments so they could claim the grant.
- It is estimated that tax concessions for superannuation contributions result in $10 billion of revenue forgone each year.

Most voluntary super contributions are made by middle- and high-income Australians.

- It has recently been announced that 'low-income earners' who contribute $1000 to their super accounts will receive an extra $1500 from the Government. Most of this will go to the part-time employed spouses of high income earners.[4]
- Changed funding arrangements for private schools mean that the Commonwealth now subsidises—to the tune of $570 million annually—people who can afford to send their children to private schools that charge fees of more than $12 000 a year.

Billions are transferred to already wealthy households, but we are told that spending on the unemployed, the sick and the elderly must be curtailed because greater public spending and public debt will lead to upward pressure on interest rates. In 1996 the first budget of Treasurer Peter Costello saved $100 million a year by abolishing the Commonwealth Dental Program. During the 2004 election campaign Prime Minister Howard announced $60 billion in new spending commitments, yet the money to fund dental care for the elderly still could not be found. How many more years of economic growth do we need before we can afford to look after aged pensioners' teeth?

The boom in middle-class welfare reflects a far-reaching transformation of politics in Australia. It reveals how our national objectives have gradually moved away from providing and improving essential services and helping those most in need to bribing the well-off for their electoral support. The apparent lack of funds for health and education is not an unfortunate fact of modern life: it is the result of a deliberate political strategy, one with bipartisan support. The rise and rise of middle-class welfare exemplifies the narrowness of political debate in Australia. Growth fetishism—the preoccupation with economic growth at the expense of other social and personal goals—is advocated by both major political parties. The ideas of nation building, investing in our children's future and protecting the most vulnerable, although preserved in the rhetoric, have vanished from the reality of modern politics. The predisposition of the middle class to define their wellbeing in terms of the things they do not possess, rather than the advantages they enjoy, is perhaps the biggest obstacle to social progress in this country.

The Beamer or the baby

Perhaps the most disquieting consequence of affluenza is the way it corrupts values. In short, market values have increasingly colonised all other values, so that ethical decisions have become economic decisions, despite a nagging feeling that putting a price on some things actually devalues them. Even the most intimate and precious aspects of being human have been subtly transformed into their antithesis. Becoming a parent used to be something we did because it was part of the human condition; now it is a 'lifestyle choice', and it is the consumer approach to parenthood that the Howard Government has appealed to with its package of 'family-friendly' taxing and spending initiatives. For many young adults the decision to have a baby is the outcome of a cost–benefit analysis. 'How much will it set us back if we have a baby?' If you add up twenty years of food, clothing, pocket money and mobile phone bills—not to mention the forgone income of the new mother, the costs of childcare, the school fees, and so on—you can only lose.

In the richest societies humanity has ever known, people are asking whether they can afford to have a baby. When today's 20- and 30-year-olds conclude they cannot, it is not because they are struggling financially. It is because, prompted by the pressures of consumerism and luxury fever, they have set themselves overly high lifestyle goals. They have come to believe they are not in a position to have a baby until they have paid off most of the mortgage, hold down two high-paying jobs, own a couple of expensive cars, and are well on the way to providing for their retirement.

People's attachment to these lifestyle goals and the sense of self acquired from achieving them is so strong they genuinely believe they cannot afford to have a baby. One might ask whether people who deploy a financial calculus in the parenthood decision are worthy of becoming parents in any case. How much unconditional commitment is a father or mother going to give to their child if they are constantly evaluating how much this small person is costing them? We hear of parents who berate their ungrateful or uncooperative children by lecturing them on how much they have had to spend to raise them.

A recent study of money and family time reported the following observation from a 17-year-old Sydney boy, Mike, who was asked whether he would prefer more time with his overworked father or more money:

> Put it this way, this day and age, it's just money. 'Cause I reckon people our age don't really hang around with their parents much. I only see my dad when he's about to go to bed. We don't spend time together that much. Maybe on a Sunday we might go for a walk at Manly, [so it's] money for sure.[5]

Mike has decided not to have children for the same reasons:

> Just think how much money you can keep for yourself. My dad
> says, 'Mike, we spend so much money on you three kids—just
> one of you costs about $250 000, just raising you . . . If you
> didn't have kids you could keep it all to yourself. Just be rich.'

Thanks, Dad. Reassuringly, some of Mike's classmates saw his attitude as selfish and extreme.

Such an approach to life exemplifies the selfishness of the consumer society, yet, for all their dewy-eyed praise of the family, it is precisely this self-centredness that our political leaders promote with their emphasis on the financial burdens facing parents. Perhaps the family-values rhetoric of conservative politicians is an attempt to conceal the fact that their economic and social policies are at the root of the decline in those values. Ironically, although the support for households with children is designed to alleviate the financial burden of family formation, the subtext of the whole debate—that having children is, and should be, a financial decision—works the other way. It is a largely unnoticed consequence of the creep of market thinking into all aspects of our personal and social lives, and it is shared both by the main political parties and by a growing proportion of the population who have known no society other than one motivated by the values of the market.

Every time a research organisation announces it has calculated that having a child will set a couple back by $300 000 (or some similarly large sum) it reinforces the idea that the decision to become a parent is a pecuniary one. A recent University of New South Wales report on the costs of having children declared, 'The price of a child is the commitment of resources required to raise a child of given "quality".' It is the relevant concept when thinking about the factors that might influence fertility decisions'. There could be no better illustration of the contradiction between the conservatives' simultaneous championing of family values and the growth-at-all-costs mentality. It is this calculus of parenthood that governments appeal to every time they talk about the 'burden' of having children.

Never mind that bearing and raising a child is one of the most profoundly human experiences, that parenthood unlocks emotions that otherwise remain untapped, and that most parents come to realise that they themselves grow up only when they become mothers or fathers. Never mind that watching your children grow and step out into the world—stumbling, suffering, achieving and flourishing—gives a parent's life a depth of interest and richness that cannot be bought for any price; that becoming a parent extends the tree of family stretching back generations; that children and grand-children can provide a sense of belonging in the world and a com-mitment to building a better society that can be had no other way. Never mind all that.

Today, the virtues of parenthood are drowned in the icy waters of financial calculation. The joys and challenges of parent-hood cannot successfully compete with the yen for a stainless steel kitchen and a holiday house. Yet government thinks it can undo decades of escalating selfishness—a change in the national character promoted by the market-based individualist policies it promotes—by offering a $3000 child bonus to tip the cost–benefit analysis in favour of the baby.

Having committed $300 000 to having a child, parents cannot be blamed for wanting a good return on their investment. Ten fingers and ten toes used to be enough, but these days parents want more: a well-balanced, loving person is not sufficient. The child must *achieve*. Hence the rise of the pushy parent, imbuing children with a desperation to achieve, defining their life goals from the cradle, identifying their extraordinary talents, and dragging them from sporting field to gym and from music lesson to cram school. The tragedy is that if the goal is to guide our children towards fulfilled lives these efforts are doomed to fail.

There is now a large amount of psychological literature showing that people who pursue extrinsic goals lead less happy lives than people who pursue intrinsic goals. So those who set their sights on money, fame and the envy of others are much less likely to be happy than those whose goals are stronger relationships, a sense of personal fulfilment and stronger ties with the community. Alas, the child's contentment is often sacrificed to the egos of the parents.

Materialism against values

Public awareness of the cost of consumer lifestyles has given rise to a growing unease—an inner conflict between what we do daily and what we believe is right for us and our society. New research commissioned for this book shows a large majority of Australians believe that escalating materialism has harmful effects on parents, children and communities. The December 2004 survey, of over 1600 people, found that 80 per cent agreed with the proposition 'Most Australians buy and consume far more than they need: it's wasteful' (see Table 3). This view is strongly held across age and income groups. The strength of concern about the impacts of materialism stands in odd contrast to the belief expressed by nearly two-thirds of the population, that they cannot afford to buy everything they really need. Although most Australians believe other Australians buy more than they need, they also think they themselves are going without. Most of us can recognise the symptoms of affluenza in others but not in ourselves.

There is similar concern about the effects of materialism in the United States. A report prepared for the Merck Family Fund in 1995

TABLE 3: Australians' attitudes to materialism and values: percentage agreeing with statement

Statement	Total	Couples without children	Couples with children	Single parents	Living alone
Most Australians buy and consume far more than they need: it's wasteful.	80	79	82	80	77
Too many Australians are focused on working and making money and not enough on family and community.	75	70	82	83	68
Our materialistic society makes it harder to instil positive values in our children.	79	80	74	88	87
There should be more limits on advertising to children.	86	87	88	84	87

delivered a devastating attack on American consumerism. *Yearning for Balance* described the results of a detailed investigation, carried out by means of a national survey and focus groups, of US citizens' perspectives on consumption and the American way of life.[6] It found that Americans believe the value system that dominates their society is wrong: 'They believe materialism, greed, and selfishness increasingly dominate life, crowding out a more meaningful set of values centered on family, responsibility, and community'. The vast majority want their lives to be based on the values of family closeness, friendship and individual and social responsibility but believe their society is far from achieving that. They want to achieve a balance between the material and non-material sides of their lives.

Australians feel the same way. In a 1999 survey Australians were asked what it would take to improve their personal quality of life. Large majorities nominated as 'very important' more time with family and friends (75 per cent) and less stress and pressure (66 per cent); a minority nominated more money to buy things (38 per cent).[7] Another survey, conducted in 2002 by Newspoll, asked respondents whether they agreed or disagreed with the statement that 'Australian society today is too materialistic, with too much emphasis on money and not enough on the things that really matter'.[8] Overall, 83 per cent of respondents agreed. The proportions agreeing with the statement were remarkably stable across the income distribution (see Figure 13)—with the exception of the richest households, where 'only' 69 per cent agreed that Australia is too materialistic. Women were more likely to agree that we are too materialistic, although the difference was not great: 87 per cent compared with 79 per cent of men. No differences were apparent between families with and without children. The survey question itself gives us pause to ask what 'the things that really matter' are. Richard Eckersley's work provides a persuasive answer: for most people the things that really matter are relationships with family and friends and time to do the things that are personally fulfilling.

The new survey commissioned for this book uncovered widespread concern about the effects of overwork on the quality of family life. Seventy-five per cent of Australians agree with the proposition 'Too many Australians are focused on working and making money and not enough on family and community' (see Table 3). Once again, with the exception of respondents aged more than 70 years, this view is held strongly across income and age groups. In the over-70s group only 62 per cent of respondents agreed. Women are somewhat more likely to agree that Australians sacrifice family for work and money: 78 per cent compared with 72 per cent of men.

Australians seem particularly troubled about the corrupting effect of materialism on children. The new survey asked whether our materialistic society makes it harder to instil positive values in our children; 79 per cent of respondents agreed. Older people hold this view more strongly than younger adults. However, parents with children aged less than five years seem to be a little less concerned: the percentage agreeing with the proposition was 10 per cent lower than the national average. But this attitude does not survive the maturing of their children: among parents with children aged twelve to fifteen years, 88 per cent believe that materialism makes positive values harder to instil. As their children grow up, parents become painfully aware of the influence on their children's values of forces outside the home. Once peers, musicians and the media begin to influence adolescent behaviour, it seems parental concern with materialism increases substantially. Single parents are the most anxious group.

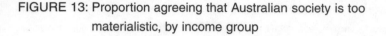

FIGURE 13: Proportion agreeing that Australian society is too materialistic, by income group

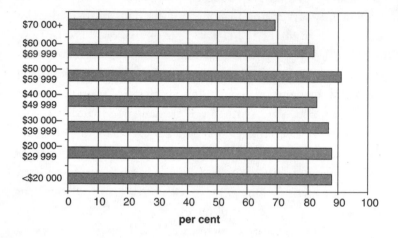

The new survey also sought opinions on one way of limiting materialism's influence on children. Eighty-six per cent of respondents agreed that there should be more limits on advertising to children, including 47 per cent who strongly agreed. Only 4 per cent of respondents disagreed. This widespread desire to put barriers between advertisers and children undoubtedly reflects the big increase in advertisers' efforts to target children.

Regardless of whether they are parents or not, Australians believe that materialism is harmful to children and that simple steps such as curbing advertising should be taken. Typically, the response of governments and the advertising industry is to suggest that parents take more individual responsibility for what their children are exposed to. But parents cannot opt out of society; they cannot control everything their children see and do; and nor do they want to. Parents feel overwhelmed by the responsibilities governments impose on them and know that taking collective action to protect their children is the best way to make a difference. When governments refuse to accept responsibility for providing collective solutions, they ensure that the problem will persist.

Nowhere is this better illustrated than in young people's access to pornography. Research shows that the level of 16- and 17-year-olds' access to Internet pornography is high and that they view material so offensive even adults in Australia cannot legally see it on video.[9] When presented with polling showing that 93 per cent of parents of teenagers want governments to take responsibility for the problem and require Internet service providers to filter content, both the Liberal Party and the Labor Party respond that parents should take responsibility for their children's conduct. The financial interest of the Internet industry is put before the emotional health of Australia's young people.

Perhaps the persistence of the battler myth is linked to parents' anxiety about corrupting influences on their children. Governments in the thrall of market ideology refuse to regulate particular commercial activities and instead assign responsibility to parents, but then they are willing to apply a balm for these social ills in the form of tax cuts and middle-class welfare. Rather than stepping in to help parents with the real battles they face, they transform moral concerns into financial anxieties. Of course, it cannot work in the longer term: the balm applied cannot mask the type of pain felt.

The responses to the various surveys discussed here show a large proportion of Australians believe that they do not have enough money *and* that society places too much emphasis on money and material goods. This suggests a disjunction between people's immediate assessment of their own financial position, which tends to be self-focused and income-driven, and their recognition that society in general is too materialistic and motivated by money instead of 'the things that really matter'. Australians are deeply ambivalent about the contradiction. They can see that affluenza is eating away at society, yet they are too fearful to change their behaviour in any meaningful way. They are wedded to 'financial security', even though they know that non-material aspirations are the ones that will bring them contentment.

Most people seem unable to change course and introduce more balance into their lives, despite suspecting that a simpler life would probably be a happier one. This suspicion is borne out by a number of studies of the relationship between materialism and quality of life. In one Australian study the authors defined 'materialism' as a value with three components: the centrality of acquisition in a person's life, the role of possessions in defining success, and the contribution of material things to the pursuit of happiness. The study confirmed the results of overseas work, finding a negative relationship between materialism and life satisfaction: '. . . those individuals who were high in materialism were less satisfied with their "life as a whole" and with specific "life domains" than those who were low in materialism'.[10]

There is one large group of Australians who have proved willing to defy convention, ignore social pressure and cast off the values of consumerism that so limit their choices. These are the downshifters.

Chapter 10
The downshifters

*In the last ten years have you **voluntarily** made a long-term change in your lifestyle, other than planned retirement, which has resulted in you earning less money? For example, have you voluntarily changed to a lower paying job, reduced your work hours, or quit work to study or stay at home?*

———question from Newspoll survey of downshifting

When ABC Television launched *SeaChange* in 1999 it had no idea how popular the program would become. The program appears to have captured and reflected a shared dream of city dwellers—to leave the rat race and live a slower, simpler life in which relationships and personal satisfaction take priority over material and career success.

Downshifters are people who have made a conscious decision to accept a lower income and a lower level of consumption in order to pursue other life goals. They are motivated by a desire for more balance in their lives, more personal fulfilment and more time with their families. Some qualify as 'real estate refugees', driven out of the cities by rising house prices and the pressure to work longer and harder to repay onerous mortgages. Many do not even move house; they just change the way they live their lives.

Before downshifting, there was a long history of 'voluntary simplicity', perhaps best represented in Australia by the communities in and around Nimbin in northern New South Wales. Downshifters are sometimes caricatured as new-age dreamers— hippies, greenies and vegans who have opted out. If this were ever a true picture of downshifters, it is certainly false now. For a start, there are just too many of them. At a time when market ideology and consumerism appear to have a more powerful grip than ever before, the decision to swim against the tide seems to have become a mainstream one. We are much more likely to find a downshifter living quietly next door than in a combi van.

Who are they?

In 2002 a nationwide survey found that 23 per cent of adults in their 30s, 40s or 50s had downshifted during the preceding ten years[1]: that is nearly a quarter of Australians in that age range. Given the pressure to define success in terms of increasing incomes and displays of consumer goods, it is astonishing to find that such a large proportion of the population has rejected the materialist preoccupations of Australian society and chosen to emphasise other, non-material aspects of life.

The survey found that downshifters are about equally likely to be in their 30s, 40s or 50s (see Figure 14), that men are a little more likely to downshift than women, and that households with children are just as likely to downshift as those without. Proportionally, there are more downshifters living in the cities than outside of them, although the difference is not great. This is interesting: the pressures of city living could be expected to

FIGURE 14: Proportion who are downshifters, by age

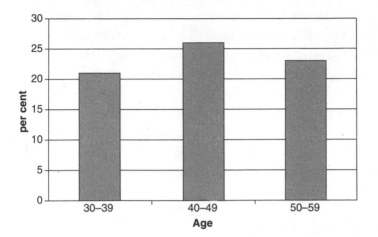

result more often in a decision to downshift. Some downshifters, the sea-changers, do move out of the cities as a consequence of these stresses but not in numbers sufficient to exceed those who remain.

It is widely believed that the downshifting phenomenon is confined to the affluent middle class, either because they have a large enough asset base to be able to take the risk or because they are more likely to hold 'post-materialist' values. But the evidence shows this not to be the case. Downshifters are not confined to wealthy and middle-income households (see Figure 15), and there is no appreciable difference in the prevalence of downshifting among white- and blue-collar workers. The household incomes shown in Figure 15 are, however, those reported by respondents after their change in lifestyle, and it is reasonable to assume the incomes had fallen as a result of the change. While the drop in income ranges from 10 per cent to 100 per cent, on average down-shifters in Britain report a 40 per cent drop[2]; the figure is probably similar in Australia.

There are four main methods of downshifting: 29 per cent choose to reduce their working hours; 23 per cent change to a lower paying job; 19 per cent stop work; and 19 per cent change careers. Why do downshifters make the change? More than a third of them say they have done so mainly because they want to spend more time with their families—an intention supported by other studies, which show that a large majority of Australians say that, instead of more income, more time with family and less stress would make them happier. The next most important motive is a healthier lifestyle (23 per cent), followed by a desire for more personal fulfilment (16 per cent) and a more balanced lifestyle (16 per cent)—see Figure 16. The importance of a healthier lifestyle is

FIGURE 15: Proportion who are downshifters, by income

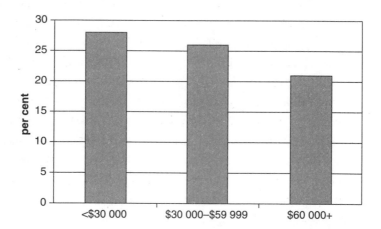

FIGURE 16: Why Australians downshift

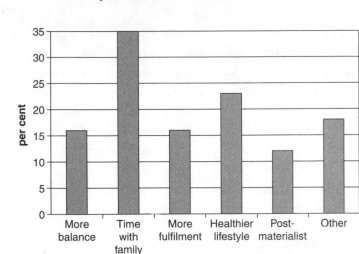

consistent with anecdotal evidence that serious health scares, such as a heart attack or a cancer diagnosis, sometimes lead to radical life changes.

Few downshifters appear to be motivated primarily by post-materialist values: only 12 per cent nominated 'a less materialistic' or 'a more environmentally friendly' lifestyle as their main reason. However, the decision to downshift usually involves a complex mix of reasons, including personal motives and matters of principle. Women are more likely to nominate more time with family and a more balanced approach to life, while men are more likely to mention a healthier lifestyle as their main reason. All income groups emphasise more time with family, although high-income downshifters are much more likely to stress personal fulfilment and those on low incomes a healthier lifestyle.

Their stories

The statistics tell us about the extent of downshifting and some of the broad motivations, but they do not give us a feel for what the experience is really like. A more recent study examined the phenomenon through detailed interviews with twenty downshifters and discussions with three focus groups made up of some people who had downshifted and some who had not.[3]

Every downshifter's story is different, but some themes do emerge. When asked about the circumstances in their lives that led to their decision, the downshifters emphasise four main reasons: the desire to have a more balanced life; a clash between personal values and the values of their workplaces; a quest for personal fulfilment; and health concerns. Typically, they make the decision for a combination of these reasons, and for most it was a considered and gradual process.

Several factors do, however, operate to make the decision to change more difficult. Many people are preoccupied with providing for their children, giving them a head start in life in ways that can be expensive. This factor can work at a subtle level—for example, when parents want their children to be able to match their peers in living standards and access to 'stuff'. But more obvious factors also come into play. Many parents feel obliged to work long and hard in order to afford private schooling and to put their children through university without a HECS debt at the end. In some cases, shared responsibility for children from previous relationships acts as a constraint. One couple talked of the cost of maintaining three families (both had been married before) and the consequent pressure to work harder. 'My assets have been divided twice due to separation,' said the male partner.

Their combined income would put them in the top 10 per cent of Australian households.

The sense of responsibility to children, and sometimes to other family members, is often enough to cause potential down-shifters to decide against it. Some who have not made the change describe downshifting as 'selfish'. For them, the decision is seen as one taken for one's own sake, to give oneself an easier life. But downshifters with children never see it in these terms: they see themselves as giving *more* to their families but measure the gift in terms of time and affection rather than money. As one down-shifter said, 'A BMW won't give you a hug or draw you a picture'.

One of the dominant themes to emerge in connection with the decision not to downshift is the heightened level of financial insecurity felt by many people (especially those in their 40s and 50s), often related to perceptions about retirement. This is curious when one considers that Australians are richer than they have ever been and that we have had over a decade of sustained economic growth. When asked why they do not downshift, many people nominate 'fear' or 'anxiety'. Some admit they could downshift if they wanted to but that the prospect of such a change is too scary. As this suggests, people who do make the break frequently have to be courageous, which explains why the change often comes only after some years of deliberation and can be precipitated by a sudden, unpleasant change in circumstances, such as a new boss, ill health or a business in difficulty.

Seeking balance

Many downshifters cite as their principal motive the difficulty of constantly juggling life's competing demands and the stresses this generates in their personal lives. Some speak of the relentless pressure to 'get it all done', which is invariably associated with combining work and family roles. The wish to spend more time with children is another strong motive. Paul, a 44-year-old, worked long hours in television in Sydney and was often overseas for weeks at a time. When his first child was born he realised his job was incompatible with his desire to spend at least some time with his family:

> With the birth of our first child I realised there was much more to life than just working non-stop. But the job demanded being available 24 hours a day, seven days a week ... I could see colleagues' marriages breaking up. I didn't want this to be me. So I made the decision not to apply for positions like these again.

Fifty-year-old Leah asked for more flexible hours at the art gallery where she worked as a curator, so that she could care for her two young children. She was refused:

> Their so-called family-friendly approach was illustrated when I had to bring my children in to a staff meeting called unexpectedly, only to be told children were not allowed in the staff room. So after eighteen years of working there I'd had enough.

While some downshifters equate a more balanced life with being able to spend more time with their families, others want more time to pursue personal interests or just to slow down and live less frenetically. For Zelda, living in a more measured way entailed leaving Sydney for a town near the north coast of New South Wales:

It took me about six months to wind down and slow down. Now we live life more slowly; there is time to make things, grow things and savour things. It was absolutely the right decision not just because there's more time for things and each other. Luke and I would never have been able to afford a house in Sydney and didn't really want our children to grow up in such a rushed and materialistic environment.

When 35-year-old Damien changed from working long hours in the corporate sector to a job in the charity sector he was seeking more balance: 'I have time to pursue things that I believe in and that I'm passionate about as part of my day-to-day job, as opposed to being something that I had to squeeze in as part of my work life in the corporate sector, when there was never any time.'

A clash of values

Another important motive for downshifting is the clash between the personal values of the downshifter and those of their workplace. Changes in workplace culture and management practices, and the intensification of work in recent years, are at the heart of many decisions to change. Downsizing, outsourcing, longer work hours and the faster pace of work have all put more pressure on people and contributed to a lower quality of life. One refugee from big business observed, 'I see the corporate world as carnivorous. The pecking order is unhealthy and quite savage. I found it morally bankrupt.' Another said he got out because 'the moral structure of the business was wrong'. Other people said they could no longer tolerate the incessant demands to 'do the deals', 'bring in the business' and increase 'billable hours'. And another said, 'It is easy to lose consciousness of decisions, to lose the ability to choose. You become complicit in the culture.'

This feeling of loss of control over one's life is a theme that consistently emerges with downshifters. The more people feel they have lost control, and the more serious the personal and moral consequences, the more likely they are to move into radically different kinds of jobs—in areas such as the helping professions, the environment and charities. David, aged 59, worked in Sydney as a senior manager for a multinational corporation for many years until he downshifted at the end of 2000. He explained the circumstances of his working life at the time and the clash between his personal values and those of the corporation:

> The company was going through a horror stretch which they described as restructuring or 'right sizing', but this actually meant massive job losses. It was not a pleasant place to be, especially as I had a key role in the process of getting rid of people. But on a personal level, I was sick of the hours (at least 12 hours a day), sick of the traffic and especially turned off by the new culture and values of the company. They brought in the 'head-kickers' from overseas.

Twenty-seven-year-old Alistair worked in a leading law firm for a number of years but left for a very different job in the non-government sector in a developing country:

> I always knew it wasn't me, not my values . . . You see all those people who get to the top and you're turned off. When it comes down to it, it's a business, all about you billing the client and earning money, recording every six minutes and making money for the firm. This concept is inimical to my nature.

Others just realise they are in the wrong profession: 'I remember it was at my boss's retirement party when I was just about to turn 30 and he had turned 60. I remember looking at him and thinking, "My God, I can't do this for another 30 years". The things that I was feeling—the stress, the discontentment, the disgruntlement—he was still feeling at 60.'

Affluenza induces people to put their own financial interests above everything else, and that often means moral doubts are pushed aside. For downshifters, these doubts gnaw away at them, perhaps for years, before they decide they are not willing to sell their soul any more.

Seeking contentment

Another theme in the downshifters' narrative is the desire to make a change for what might be called existential reasons. They seek some form of inner contentment or, as one downshifter put it, 'I wanted congruence between what I do in the world and what I am in myself.' Invariably, the decision-making process is gradual and characterised by a great deal of reflection about why they feel unfulfilled in both their working and their personal lives. The journey is often difficult, sometimes causing disappointment among family members, but in each case these downshifters have found a way of living that brings greater self-acceptance and psychological wellbeing.

Franco thought a lot about the failure of material possessions to bring him any sense of fulfilment:

Once, when I was negotiating with my boss about work, I realised I didn't want more money to motivate me. I was looking for more challenges, more responsibility, a certain type of work, and I was more than willing to sacrifice money for it. I worked this way for quite a few years and felt much better. I wasn't interested in the power politics and the money-making parts of work.

Another, a 59-year-old senior public servant, felt dissatisfied for many years in both his work and his personal life. After much searching, questioning and reflection he concluded, 'I no longer wanted to live in the milieu of high income, high expenditure, owning all sorts of things; of getting up in the morning to load yourself with the electronics and technology and getting out there and networking for whatever purpose . . . and the long hours.' So he quit.

Health

Many downshifters nominate health as the factor that stimulated them to make the change. In some cases it is an accumulation of stress over time. One person described the effect of long hours and pressure: 'I was losing weight, my hair was falling out, I wasn't sleeping. It was getting to the stage where it was really affecting my health and I knew I had to do something, that something had to change.' For other people, it was a case of their health suddenly breaking down. Forty-six-year-old Andrea, who ran an IT consultancy with her husband, lived a life dominated by work as 'contract after contract rolled in'. There was little time for leisure, relaxation or personal reflection. 'I dressed up in the corporate suits, went in there pretty aggressively, got the work done.' After eight years of living and working this way, Andrea suffered a breakdown: 'There were many things that caused it. Work was getting more and more stressful, but an argument with my step-daughter threw me over the edge. I had to have treatment, somehow managed to finish the current contract and then we left for a holiday.'

Fiona also experienced exhaustion and anxiety after years of supporting her partner in his own business. At the end of 2002 they decided to close down the business because they both felt they desperately needed a change: 'I felt an absolute stressed out mess, as if I'd lost my whole personality and self completely . . . We both wanted to do something different. Bruce wanted to work fewer hours and have less work stress. We'd paid off our house, our kids were grown up, so we felt we were in a position to live on less.'

How does life change?

People who choose to downshift usually stress that they are not dropping out of society. As one of them explained, 'We are actually creating something new, not getting out'. A change in patterns of consumption is an important step in the downshifting process. After assessing how much they consume and how much they actually need, people find it easier to change their work and consumption patterns. When asked what they do without, the downshifters' responses are remarkably uniform. All said they eat out less often and, when they do, they choose less expensive restaurants. Indeed, food features prominently in many discussions of new lifestyles. Most downshifters say they spend more time cooking and enjoy doing so. Many say they are much more careful about the food they buy, and some take pleasure in growing their own vegetables. This is partly motivated by tighter budgets, but it also reflects a new emphasis on healthy eating.

Almost all downshifters give up expensive holidays, including holidays abroad. None of those interviewed expressed regret about this; some said they just take cheaper holiday options in Australia.

On the other hand, some younger downshifters take the opportunity to use some of their new-found time to travel, especially to developing countries to experience life as it is lived by others.

Surprisingly, another frequently mentioned type of forgone consumption is spending on clothes needed for work—the corporate uniforms that are no longer needed. Downshifters often gleefully talk of discarding their suits: such clothing seems to symbolise the life they left behind.

Andrea, whose income fell dramatically after she and her husband wound up their business, summed up many of these changes: 'We feel better, we grow our own vegies, we cook more. I no longer spend $1000 on each corporate outfit. We have fewer restaurant meals now, make our own beer, don't go on overseas trips anymore. We have a better, healthier lifestyle.'

In addition to doing without these items of expenditure, many downshifters take a completely different approach to spending. Although much less preoccupied with money, they are nevertheless more careful about how they dispose of what they have. One described himself and his partner as 'aware buyers' who are rarely tempted to buy things they don't need. Others avoid shopping centres whenever possible and are not tempted to spend their leisure time window shopping or engaged in retail therapy. Some adopt a conscious strategy of avoiding exposure to affluenza sufferers; others make it clear that they will control their money rather than having it control them. They become 'conscious consumers', rather than impulse buyers, and so put themselves beyond the reach of the marketers.

Downshifters with children often talk about how their offspring adjust to lower household incomes. Some seem to 'protect' their children from the changes, either by keeping up spending on items specific to the children or by postponing the decision to downshift until the children are well into their teens. Others say there is more discretion than is commonly believed:

> We basically set about minimising our expenditure, and that wasn't that hard with kids. Strangely enough everyone thinks it costs a fortune . . . All of our friends were going to private hospitals and had private health insurance . . . I didn't think there was anything wrong with the public system and we had our first baby at the local public hospital.

He walks his children to school each day, avoiding travel expenses and spending that extra time with them.

Some downshifters adjust to their new financial circumstances quickly, but others have difficulty. For most, the dominant change in their lives involves taking control of their time and devoting it to more satisfying activities. This often means more time with partners and children, particularly when children are young. Many report that they spend much more time outdoors engaged in physical activity. Comments about how much healthier they feel are common; they see themselves as fitter and more invigorated. Some say the life change precipitated an instant lifting of mood and a new approach to life. Leah said she felt an enormous sense of relaxation once she downshifted: 'A lot of bullshit just disappeared. It was like being in another world, and I couldn't understand how I had been in that environment for so long. I suddenly had a clear view.'

Another downshifter who at 30 left a promising career in a big law firm to become a photographer, urged caution: 'I think it's important to make the point that downshifting is not "a one size fits all" solution.'

How others react

Public attitudes to people who decide to make radical life changes in pursuit of greater contentment are mixed. The difference between downshifters' motives and the reactions of some of those around them reflects the fundamental feature of the downshifting phenomenon—a change in personal values, such that financial and material success is no longer the dominant motive. This spills over into everyday reactions. A young mother from Gosford told of how her friends are 'amazed' when they discover she does not own a microwave oven. There is a powerful, indeed overwhelming, assumption that everyone is committed to acquiring the best material lifestyle they reasonably can. It's just how life in Australia is, and bemusement and expressions of derision are typical responses to downshifters' decisions to flout this convention.

The spread of affluenza and market values reflects and reinforces a broader social movement towards individualism. Political leaders have promised more 'choice' and say they want to transfer responsibility from government to individuals. But it seems that only particular forms of individuality are acceptable, so that people who make the choice to reject the dominance of market values are characterised as irresponsible.

Most downshifters say the reactions of their friends and family are diverse; a few say they have received nothing but support. Many report that their friends and family are shocked when they make the change and that they are often told they must be 'nuts'. At the same time, almost all downshifters note that many of their friends and colleagues have expressed curiosity and envy. Alastair said, 'The week before I left the law firm I had a stream of people coming into the office, closing the door and going "OK, tell me how you did it? What websites did you visit, who do I call?"' Paul, who now runs his own outdoors business, said, 'A lot of my friends and colleagues have been very jealous . . . Everyone keeps saying "You're so lucky", they just keep saying "Don't come back".'

Negative reactions can be intensified by cultural expectations. In her early 30s, Sasha abandoned her career as a medical professional to become a counsellor. She had to withstand intense criticism from her parents, who had grown up on the Indian subcontinent and were plagued by an acute form of deferred happiness syndrome: 'They thought I was just weak and running away from my problems . . . Their attitude was: "Well you're not supposed to be happy. Work is work, and it pays the rent. You have all these nice things. What's wrong with you? What more do you want?"'

One consistent observation is that the decision to change causes downshifters to sort out their true friends from the ones who don't really matter to them. As Andrea said, 'I think the changes we've made to our lives have really shown who our friends are. The people who we now look on as acquaintances think we're mad, but our real friends have said "Good on you". It's been very interesting to see who in the community has been supportive.'

Downshifters often move into a new social environment. They drift away from some of their friends and work colleagues because their lives are now different and because the decision to downshift can uncover some underlying value conflicts: 'My friends changed a lot, as they no longer had the same values as me,' said one. Sometimes they also find it difficult to explain to relatives and friends what they are doing and why. This is partly because until recently in Australia downshifters have felt that their decisions were made in isolation. One said it took a long time to explain her decision to her siblings, partly because the term 'downshifting' was not used at the time.

Studies have identified a loss of status as something many downshifters must confront, particularly downshifters who make dramatic changes to their lives. Many seem to have prepared themselves for this loss of status: after all, one of the obstacles to making the decision is the fear of losing standing among one's peers and the community, and income and associated lifestyle are perhaps the most important markers of status. Andrea summed up the feelings of some about their loss of status:

> Only in the eyes of people who don't matter. There are certainly people who now look down their noses at us, but in terms of our real friends and ourselves quite the opposite. I think we've actually gained a lot of respect from people who'd love to do the same thing but haven't got the guts. Certainly in our eyes we're prouder of ourselves because we've done what we really wanted to do, not kowtowed to society.

Difficulties and delights

The nationwide survey of downshifters found that nearly 90 per cent are happy with the change in their lifestyle, although 38 per cent said they miss the extra income and 17 per cent admitted that, despite being happy with the change, they have found losing the income very tough.

When asked about the difficulties they experienced as a result of downshifting, respondents usually mentioned financial concerns first. Some said they worry at times about whether they will be able to provide for their retirement. For many downshifters, at least among those who make more extensive changes, there is an early period of adjustment. Some miss the ability to indulge in certain forms of 'luxury' spending—such as, in one case, being able to buy presents for friends—or to have the occasional 'splurge'. In other words, the spontaneity that having plenty of money permits is replaced by financial discipline. Downshifters change the way they think about household finances. Andrea put it this way: 'The only real difficulty is when bills come in and you think, "How am I going to juggle this one?" I wouldn't actually say it was a difficulty, rather something that has to be managed. It's become easier and easier as I've become better at it.'

Most downshifters find they have to be more careful with their spending, to plan more effectively, and to be more disciplined in that aspect of their lives. One can say, though, that the anxiety they feel about a substantial reduction in income is remarkably mild considering the importance society attaches to financial security. Downshifting is charcterised by a psychological transformation, in which money and material things are relegated to a much diminished position on the list of life's priorities. In other words, adopting a different relationship to money is an essential part of the 'contract' downshifters have with themselves.

Other changes present challenges, too. Many downshifters find instant liberation, but for some casting off an entrenched work ethic and adjusting to a different pattern of daily life is a challenge:

Perhaps the only difficulty has been stopping the sense of guilt, because when we made the change we both felt huge guilt about sitting and having a cup of coffee at 10.30 in the morning . . . Allowing yourself to be who you really are took a lot of doing, shedding all that indoctrination and the social expectations, that was probably the toughest.

When asked to reflect on the benefits of the change, downshifters stress the relief and the new sense of personal freedom. Some talk of rediscovering the 'joy of living'. Fiona described the experience as 'exciting rather than frightening' and, although she sometimes feels exhausted, most of the time she feels 'exhilarated'. 'The sense of relief has just got better and better,' said another. And another simply said, 'I don't have to wear ties anymore'.

Many return to the theme of taking control of their lives, of being able to make real life choices. 'We now live by choice. What time will we get up? What shall we do today? We're not driven by external events,' said Andrea. For Paul, 'It's a more relaxed lifestyle, less stressful. In many ways, you're in charge of your own destiny.' Being in control of one's destiny is what the advertisements try to sell, but the 'choices' promised by the market are very limited. The weight of affluenza works against us making genuine choices about how we live our lives. Choosing between 49 different brands of olive oil is trivial. Downshifters often say the change has opened up their lives to opportunities that would previously have been closed off to them. A few find the responsibility that goes with the freedom difficult to cope with, although if this sense is too strong it seems to deter people from heading down the downshifting path in the first place.

Most talk of the slower pace of life: 'People don't have time to chat anymore, and we used to be like that too. But our whole pace of life has slowed down. I even drive more slowly now. I don't know how I ever had time to work. Now I can listen to the birds, smell the roses.' For others, the slower pace makes life less stimulating, although the time freed up can be devoted to creative and healthy pursuits such as sculpture, whale watching and bushwalking. A high proportion mention musical pursuits.

When the downshifters are asked if they have any regrets, there is a chorus of 'no'—except for a few who regret not doing it earlier. Downshifters talk of contentment, freedom and 'bliss'. A few say they sometimes worry about whether they will have enough savings in retirement. Some say they would recommend downshifting unreservedly, but most believe it is not for everyone. One cautioned people not to be 'under the illusion that the whole downshifting experience is euphoric'. Perhaps the last word on this should be left to Andrea: 'Anyone contemplating the change should be really honest with themselves. If people can't admit to themselves what they really want, and be absolutely honest, don't even attempt it.'

Retirement anxiety

When Australians talk about their hopes and fears, it is apparent that for many of them, especially those in their 40s and 50s, their life plans and objectives are dominated by the prospect of retirement. They constantly return to this theme—a sign of how anxious they feel about their ability to provide for a comfortable retirement at a time when government has made it clear that people can no longer rely on the pension to meet their needs. Expectations about the amount of income needed in retirement appear to have escalated considerably, and these self-imposed benchmarks put people under great pressure. At the same time there has been a change in perceptions of retirement where baby boomers in the professions and in managerial positions are concerned. They see no clear division between their working and post-working lives and think they will be able to wind down gradually and may never retire fully. Indeed, some see the idea of working hard to save for retirement then stopping work to enjoy the fruits of their labour as pathological. As one put it, 'If you see retirement as the end then you are doing the wrong thing'.

There is a marked difference in attitudes to retirement among people who have downshifted and people who have not. It is a difference that encapsulates the psychological shift that the life change represents. Those who would not consider downshifting, or who have considered it but lack the resolve, are often preoccupied with saving for retirement to an almost obsessive degree: as one woman in her 50s said of her husband, 'He's even made a down payment on his old-person's scooter'. For people who have downshifted, though, these worries seem to become less pressing. Questions about the insecurity of retirement generate animated responses from those who have not made the change but are often met with puzzlement or unconcern by those who have. In the words of one downshifter in his 40s, 'When I worked for [a major company] I was maniacally fixated on my superannuation account. Since resigning I no longer think about it.'

There appear to be two reasons for the new attitude. The first is that concern about financial futures is inescapable in a society preoccupied with money, but downshifting involves demoting the world of material possessions and financial security so that mental energy is directed elsewhere. It is impossible to live in the present if you are obsessed with money. The second reason is that downshifters have proven themselves more willing to take risks. Many seem to be confident that things will turn out fine, instead of building walls of security around themselves—walls that they believe might be breached in any case. Perhaps a third reason can be drawn from this: in contrast with the linear path of career progress in a chosen area, downshifters generally see their lives evolving in more fluid ways, with change and unpredictability being part of their experience.

These stories provide an insight into what it means to cure oneself of affluenza. It is not always easy, and it affects all aspects of life—relationships with family and friends, attitudes to status, the approach to daily life, planning for the future and, of course, finances. It is made more difficult because it feels like an isolated act. One of the biggest questions for the future of Australia is whether the thousands of individual acts of downshifting, in which the values and goals of the market are rejected, can be turned into a political movement that challenges consumer society at its core.

Deferrers, gratifiers, downshifters

Most Australians fall into one of three groups: deferrers, who know their overwork is damaging their relationships but hope to make up for it later on; gratifiers, who, in the pursuit of instant satisfaction want to spend as much as they can now and are willing to borrow to get it; and downshifters. The underlying motivation of deferrers and gratifiers is the same. Gratifiers want the money and what it buys now and accumulate financial debts as a result. Deferrers want the money and the life it buys later and accumulate relationship debts as a result. Both risk bankruptcy, the difference being that in one case the bailiffs come to the front door and in the other your partner might leave through it.

Downshifters, in contrast, break the imagined link between money and happiness. While deferrers 'postpone the day' until they accumulate the resources they believe they will need to live happily, downshifters 'seize the day' in order to pursue a more fulfilling life. The deferrers tend to be motivated primarily by financial security; the downshifters place less emphasis on money and more on their relationships, their health and a sense of personal contentment. Downshifters sacrifice money for time; deferrers sacrifice time for money; and gratifiers sacrifice money later for money now.

There are roughly equal numbers of deferrers and down-shifters in Australia. As noted, almost a quarter of adults aged 30 to 60 years are downshifters, while 30 per cent of full-time workers have been identified as deferrers. It is not clear how many might fit into the category of gratifiers. What is clear, though, is that deferrers, gratifiers and downshifters are not concentrated in any socio-economic group, family type or geographical area; each group comes from across the community.

Although downshifters can be thought of as people who have decided to effect a recovery from deferred happiness syndrome, it would be wrong to think that deferrers are no more than down-shifters in preparation. For the most part, downshifters are not people who can 'afford to take the risk' because they have accumu-lated extensive assets. Risk aversion is actually a characteristic of deferrers, and it takes courage to make the leap to downshifting. So, while some deferrers might reach a point where they decide to take the risk and seize the day, many, perhaps most, will continue to defer until retirement. There is anecdotal evidence that for a substantial number of people the dream of a happy life deferred until retirement is in fact never realised.

People who choose to reject the dominance of money in their own lives are often characterised as selfish, foolish or reckless. This attitude is held by many who, while recognising today's intense pressures, think people should be stoical and put up with the stresses for the sake of others. It is hard to avoid the conclusion, however, that much of this hostility betrays a dog-in-the-manger attitude: 'If I am stuck in a life of worries, stresses and overwork, everyone else should be too'. Growing numbers of Australians are deciding they will no longer allow such a view to determine their lives.

Chapter 11
A new politics

First they ignore you, then they laugh at you, then they fight you, then you win.

——Mahatma Gandhi

The affluenza spiral

The argument of this book can be summarised quite simply.

Since the early 1990s Australia has been infected by affluenza, a growing and unhealthy preoccupation with money and material things. This illness is constantly reinforcing itself at both the individual and the social levels, constraining us to derive our identities and sense of place in the world through our consumption activity. It causes us to withdraw into a world of self-centred gratification— often at the expense of those around us. It is manifest in over-consumption and luxury fever, especially in our purchasing of goods that promise to transform our actual selves into the ideal selves the market has helped us construct. The virus is spread and intensified by a vast marketing industry that exploits our insecurities and vanities in order to make us feel discontented. Apart from trying to persuade us to consume particular goods, the larger function of the industry is to persuade us that a happy life can be had through accumulating money and consuming more. Our culture has been colonised by the ideology and values of marketing.

As a result, Australians today feel materially deprived, even though they are richer than ever before; a pervasive discontent is continually reinforced by consumer culture. This cultivation of a sense of deprivation in the midst of plenty is essential to the reproduction of consumerism. For people infected by affluenza, more is never enough, yet they fail to understand that more consumption will not allay their feeling of discontent.

Affluenza harms us. First, people who are infected want to consume more than their incomes allow, so there has been extraordinary growth in consumer debt in the past decade. The ratcheting-up of lifestyle goals has been the main cause of the boom in house prices. The marketing industry promotes indebtedness as a means of getting what we want now and has persuaded us that the best way to save is to spend. This accelerates the affluenza spiral, and it cannot be sustained. Second, affluenza lies behind the epidemic of overwork in Australia: people feel they must work longer and harder to meet ever-rising aspirations. But overwork imposes severe costs on our health and our relationships and cannot be sustained. Third, the environment suffers as a result of affluenza. Despite complaining that their incomes are inadequate to satisfy their needs, most Australians spend large sums of money buying goods and services from which they derive no benefit. Useless consumption generates mountains of waste going to landfill every year. This, too, is unsustainable.

The affluenza spiral is intimately connected to these unsustainable activities—excessive indebtedness, overwork and wasteful consumption—and the resulting pressures help to explain the plague of psychological disorders, alienation and distress that characterises modern Australia. To cope, millions of Australians self-medicate with mood-altering drugs and excessive alcohol consumption. The market has, of course, responded enthusiastically to the demand for products that temporarily suppress the effects of affluenza.

Australia's political system invigorates affluenza by promoting the values of the market and by validating the sense of deprivation felt by people who are wealthy by any objective measure. This is reflected in our continuing obsession with the Aussie battler, the rise of middle-class welfare, and the trivialisation of the circumstances of the minority of Australians who are genuinely poor. Yet not far beneath the surface most of us know the affluenza treadmill is taking us nowhere. When questioned, most of us admit Australia is too materialistic and that money hunger is responsible for a steep decline in moral values.

The intensifying pressures of affluenza have prompted a backlash in the form of downshifting. Close to a quarter of people in their 30s, 40s and 50s have made the decision to reduce their incomes and place family, friends and contentment above money in determining their life goals. But downshifters face obstacles and sanctions because they have rejected market values. We need a new political philosophy.

Changing values

Most Australians, including those caught up in consumerist lifestyles, feel the prevailing value system is warped. They believe Australia has become too selfish and superficial, that people have lost touch with the more desirable standards of personal behaviour, such as self-restraint, mutual respect and generosity.

Conservatives have been much more adept than progressives at tapping into these concerns, even though in the name of choice they promote the very market values and consumerist goals that corrode the values we seek.

The yearning of most Australians for a society built on basic human values has been twisted into support for a retrograde conservative morality, including vilification of single mothers, hostility towards gay relationships, and attempts to demonise the 'undeserving' poor. The values of a decent society have been overlaid by outdated prejudices and positions based on particular religious convictions. And, responding to a pervasive sense of social disintegration, conservatives have made political gains by taking a disciplinarian stance on crime and drugs. The majority of Australians want to live in a society with greater moral certainty, stronger constraints on antisocial behaviour and clearer sexual standards; conservatives appear to offer solutions, even if those solutions are wrapped up with other positions that many find uncomfortable.

Thinkers and leaders on the progressive side of politics have become wary of the new politics of morality, seeing it as the stalking horse of conservatives whose approach is often punitive, divisive and repressive. Schooled in the ethical universe of the 1960s and 1970s, when the assertion of minority rights saw the overthrow of oppressive rules, many progressives have failed to engage with the moral concerns of the citizenry and have abandoned to those on the political right the most fertile grounds for social change. Now that the laws and norms that imposed sexual repression, limited opportunities for women and sanctioned racism have been renounced, the left has ended up standing for little more than the market economy with a bit of 'social justice' thrown in.

Defending minority rights is not a trivial task, but it should now be clear that it cannot form the basis of a progressive politics in the twenty-first century.

Nowhere are these contradictions more keenly fought out than in debates over the idea of the family. Defending 'the family' has become conservative territory, but it is time progressives muscled their way in with a new politics of relationships. Everyone wants a happy family life. Families are the source of most of the companionship, emotional support and love we experience throughout our lives; they are where we form our most enduring, caring and loyal relationships. Yet many progressive people, as if still crippled by the feminist and leftist critiques of the nuclear family, are afraid to defend the family; and, perversely, the more the moral conservatives have seized on the notion and moulded it into a romantic and reactionary caricature of the nuclear ideal of the 1950s, the more the progressives have vacated the field. This has been a political mistake.

The widespread unease with consumerism, even among the so-called aspirational classes, and the longing for a society with stronger values derives from something deeper than a perception of social decline. Like all humans, what modern Australians want above all is for their lives to have purpose. But finding meaning is not easy, especially when people are subjected to a barrage of commercial messages that promote superficiality, self-deception and laxity. Some are following a religious path, and they find growing church communities where they can, for a time at least, immerse themselves in a social environment that is welcoming, caring, joyous and devoted to a higher purpose. This explains the proliferation of evangelical Christian churches, where the corrupting influences of consumer culture can be left at the door and people can participate unselfconsciously in a celebration of being together (except in those bizarre evangelical churches that declare 'God wants you to be rich'). They can find affirmation and value in being part of a community. This is a rare experience nowadays, but it fulfils an essential human need—one that television, shopping malls and political parties cannot meet.

Progressives feel uneasy about the importation of American evangelism, for good reason: these communities lend themselves to capture by conservatives who distort the participants' desire for a stronger moral order into an assault on outsiders who deviate from 'the one true path'. But, rather than deriding the 'happy clappers' of the evangelical churches, we need to realise that it is only through understanding and accepting the urge to find something more satisfying than a consumer life that a 'politics of meaning' can be built. Responding to most people's wish to live with purpose in an ethical society ought to be the natural territory of progressives, since the sentiments that underlie this hunger are consistent with the construction of a more just, sustainable and peaceful society.

Political downshifting

The downshifting phenomenon points to a new form of politics. Here we have a large number of people who have chosen to reject consumerism and the preoccupations of the aspirational voter. They have concluded that the dogged pursuit of money and materialism comes at too high a cost, for both them and their families. Some of these people also believe that consumerism and money hunger impose social and environmental costs. Downshifters therefore reject the hitherto unquestioned assumption of Australian politics that voters respond first and foremost to the 'hip-pocket nerve'. These people might be called 'anti-aspirational voters'. Perhaps a similar number might be considered closet anti-aspirational voters, people who agree with the basic values of anti-aspirational voters but do not have the self-possession, courage or, in some cases, the wherewithal to make the transition to downshifting.

The motives of this large group of Australians are mixed. Undoubtedly, many downshifters were once 'middle-class whingers' who came to the conclusion that they would never have enough money to satisfy their 'needs' if their needs stayed ahead of their incomes and that this was a recipe for a life of discontent. So they decided to scale down their incomes and to scale down their needs even more. Downshifters reject the social norm of acquisitiveness, favouring a more balanced life for themselves and their families. For the most part—even though they might express a social critique that sees obsessive materialism as the source of much personal unhappiness and understand that Australian society is focused on consumption to an unhealthy degree—their actions are not primarily motivated by a conscious politics of post-materialism. Instead, it is a desire to step off the treadmill. They have redefined 'the good life' in a way that attaches less importance to money and material acquisition; in this sense, they represent an unorganised post-materialist social movement.

Downshifting is not confined to middle-class professionals and successful business people who can afford to cut their incomes because they have accumulated assets. Some downshifters fall into this category, but many are people with modest incomes who have simply decided to accept lower incomes, to live more simply and to spend more time doing the things they value more than paid work. They demonstrate an unusual degree of resolve because they have made a decision to resist powerful social pressures to pursue the symbols of success, as defined by consumer society. The norms of consumerism are reinforced by public images and private practice; acquisitiveness is the Zeitgeist, and the entire structure of consumerism depends on the constant creation of desire for more. The decision to downshift is all the more difficult because of the absence of everyday role models.

The emergence of a sizeable class of downshifters in Australia should challenge the main political parties to question their assumptions about what makes for a better society. It calls for a redefinition of success, since downshifters have defined successful living for themselves and their families in a way that thumbs its nose at the promises of consumerism. A preoccupation with more economic growth and higher incomes is no longer enough. Nor will it be enough for political leaders to change their rhetoric from economics to 'family-friendly' policies and concern about overwork. That is already happening, but it is a façade. Although there has been some change in the rhetoric, the promotion of consumerist values and growth at all costs continues, and these are precisely the things downshifters are turning away from. Yet governments continue to sacrifice to GDP growth the things downshifters value, and no amount of family-friendly rhetoric can conceal this. The main political parties are a long way from redefining the Australian dream in a way that accords with the ideals and actions of the downshifters.

It has been interesting to watch the right-wing commentators' reaction to the downshifting phenomenon. Downshifters are exercising their right to choose but doing so in a way that rejects market values. Neoliberals can imagine only one sort of choice—choice within the marketplace. So how do they react when some people elect to step outside the marketplace? This is not supposed to happen: the economics texts assume that everyone has an insatiable appetite for more things. One prominent right-wing economist could explain the downshifting phenomenon only by characterising these people as 'bludgers'. Although not willing to say so, neoliberals believe we each have a responsibility to make as much money as we can, that we have a duty to honour our obligations to a higher authority—that hallowed institution, the market—and that exercising our right to withdraw from the market is unacceptable.

The notion that we must subjugate our needs to a greater collective institution has more in common with socialism than liberalism. After decades of being told we will be set free if we allow the market to do what governments once did, we are now told by the neoliberals that we may not exempt ourselves from the dictates of the market. If becoming richer means becoming unhappier, that is the price we must pay. In reality, far from bludging from others or the state, downshifters tend to be independent individuals. They are inheritors of the liberal tradition—certainly as conceived by the founders of liberalism, such as John Stuart Mill and even Friedrich von Hayek. Modern-day neoliberals are looking more and more like the new oppressors.

Conscious consumption

Readers might have formed the impression that the problem we are talking about is consumption itself. If that were the case, the only answer would be a truly radical simplification of life. A few have taken this path—including those who make up the voluntary simplicity movement—and they seem to derive great satisfaction and purpose from living according to their convictions. But the problem is not consumption itself: the problem is our *attachment* to consumption, the way we invest our hopes, our goals and our sense of self in the things we buy and own. The problem is not so much that we consume but that we consume for the wrong reasons. Advertisers know they would sell less if they were merely to present the facts about a product, so they devote themselves to persuading us to form attachments to products because we want to use them to build an ideal self. People who have a better understanding of themselves and are less prone to self-deception can see through marketers' attempts to deceive them. They are much less vulnerable to the affluenza virus.

Conscious consumption, as opposed to no consumption, is the antidote to affluenza. Conscious consumption involves cultivating an awareness of why we buy things and understanding what needs we are trying to meet by buying this item or that one. We are more likely to recognise that a purchase will not really answer a need if we understand that our motivation is a response to marketers persuading us that a product can fill an emotional gap in our lives or project to the world an image of how we wish to be seen because we are not happy with who we are. Such an insight might cause us to buy something different (perhaps without a brand imbued with social meaning) or not buy at all. One of the first stages in the therapeutic process for compulsive shoppers is to teach them to distinguish between needs and wants. This is also the essential idea behind conscious consumption, which means refusing to allow our lives to be governed by money and the things it can buy. This is not to say that sometimes shopping can't be fun, but the first signs of self-deception and addiction must call forth the conscious consumer.

One of the most valuable things parents can do for their children is teach them to adopt a critical attitude towards marketers' attempts to influence them. Children are exposed to advertisements before they can talk. Parents who not only control the amount of television their children watch but also take the time to watch it with them and point out that advertisers are trying to deceive them help instil in those children a capacity to shield themselves from the blandishments of the market. Restrictions on advertising to children would make parents' task much easier.

Conscious consumption is an essential protective shield in our personal lives, but it must go beyond the cultivation of an awareness of our own needs and of marketers' efforts to appeal to our insecurities. We must also be conscious of the impact of our decisions on the rest of the world. We could, after all, say to ourselves, 'Yes, I have carefully considered my reasons for buying this giant gas-guzzling 4WD and decided that I really do need it'. We need to think about our consumption decisions socially as well as personally. We also need to think about our investment decisions in this way. Nearly all adult Australians have superannuation accounts: we can have our funds managed for the highest financial return, without any regard to the social and environmental consequences, or we can place our money in one of the rapidly growing ethical investment trusts, knowing our money will be put to purposes that do not damage the natural environment or result in exploitation.

The marketing industry will seize on any social trend and try to exploit it to sell more products, and it is not shy about trying to turn anticonsumption trends into their opposite. For marketers, conscious consumers are just another demographic whose psychology must be dissected in order to know how best to get them to spend against their judgment. One US market research company can declare without any suggestion of irony or embarrassment:

> For the first time in their lives, young Americans are faced with international criticism of the United States for its 'wasteful and self-indulgent' way of life. In response they are becoming less concerned with maintaining their 'hipster' lifestyles and more focused upon what is truly meaningful to them and to the world at large.
>
> Young adults, determined to reject their Baby Boomer parents' era of conspicuous consumption, have for some time been practicing selective consumption, choosing products that achieve individual expression or statements of luxury and discrimination. Now many are engaging in 'Conscious Consumption', making brand choices that offer meaning and substance.[1]

The Diesel clothing company has marketed itself as the brand worn by the antiglobalisation generation, and chains of coffee shops deck themselves out in 'Third World chic'. Of course, proving one's conscious consumption credentials by buying a branded product is oxymoronic, but that would not be the only form of moronic behaviour provoked by the marketers.

Modern corporations dislike fickle consumers, which is why so much effort goes into creating brand loyalty. Outside the market, 'loyalty' refers not to habit but to the willingness to stick by your friend or your country out of a sense of duty or love. Marketers succeed when we adopt their product as an aspect of how we define ourselves, so brand loyalty is nothing more than a form of self-love. Being loyal to a brand means we have abandoned our critical faculties and are willing to continue to buy that brand no matter whether it meets our real needs or not. Consuming consciously requires us to cultivate brand *disloyalty*—to feel no emotional commitment to a brand or a product because we no longer define ourselves by the things we buy.

We argue that the problem is not so much consumption itself but our attachment to consumption, the way our lives become bound up with and determined by the things we buy. This is not, however, the complete picture: when it comes to protection of the natural environment, consumption itself is the problem because its growth results in more waste and pollution. Reducing our consumption levels and radically changing the pattern of consumption will be inescapable in the years to come. Nevertheless, conscious consumption, which by definition means less consumption, is valuable for its own sake. It turns out that changing our consumption behaviour in the pursuit of improved wellbeing has the added benefit of contributing to the preservation of the natural world.

We have talked only about individual responses to affluenza. But, because the forces that must be resisted are so powerful and ubiquitous, we need to act as citizens as well as individuals. We need a political response to affluenza. Before we make some final comments on such a politics, though, it is worth reiterating that in stressing affluence we are not dismissing poverty.

Poverty amid plenty

Conservative economists and institutions such as the World Bank have long argued that the best way to look after the poor in developing countries is to facilitate economic growth by liberalising economies everywhere—free trade, free flow of foreign capital, privatising public assets, and so on. They say it is counterproductive to try to solve poverty directly and that governments hurt everyone when they try to tackle poverty by taking from the rich to give to the poor. (If Robin Hood had taken Economics 101 at the University of Nottingham he would undoubtedly have sided with the Sheriff.) Instead, the argument has it, if the economy can be made to grow faster some of the benefits will 'trickle down' to the poor and that is the best way to help them.

Although developed with respect to poor countries, the trickle-down argument has in recent decades been applied to countries such as Australia too. Of course, social democrats have called for, and in some cases implemented, redistributive policies, but across the world parties of the left have conceded that the primary objective of government should be to maximise the growth rate of GDP and that free markets are the best way to do this. In place of trickle down, the slogans have been 'a rising tide raises all boats' and 'social inclusion'. In 2003 Peter Mandelson, often seen as British Labour Prime Minister Tony Blair's Svengali, wrote in *The Times*: 'We are all Thatcherites now, at least in our economic policies'. This could equally be said of the Australian Labor Party.

After decades of growth we still have poverty. About 10 per cent of Australian households fit any reasonable definition of 'poverty' and perhaps another 10 per cent seriously struggle at various points in their lives. Of the rest, perhaps half would say they are struggling—and not just the bottom half—although few would be able to look the average East Timorese in the eye and complain about their financial situation. Concern for the under-privileged is right: a society in which no one cared for others would be a type of hell. But this necessary compassion should not provide the motive for a politics of social change in a society where the great majority of people are surrounded by abundance. Clinging to the deprivation model actually reinforces the arguments and political position of conservatives—the growth fetishists—and prevents us from confronting poverty. The deprivation model is simply the obverse of the growth model: they are both obsessed by income.

In Australia we do not lack the ability to solve poverty; we lack the will. And the richer we become as a society the more unwilling we are to sympathise with those at the bottom of the heap. We have been unable to make the necessary changes to social structures to reduce poverty because of the majority's preoccupation with protecting their own incomes, a preoccupation nurtured every time a political party declares that its priority is more growth. The goal of full employment has consistently been sacrificed to the interests of higher incomes for the wealthy. In a society where too much is not enough, social justice is an impossible goal.

To solve the problem of poverty, real deprivation, we must first solve the problem of affluence, imagined deprivation. Yet that must be done in the face of the formidable pressures applied by consumerism itself, which, having solved poverty materially, must constantly recreate it psychologically. Otherwise, the system cannot keep functioning, because the role of marketing is to sell the belief in one's own deprivation and the redemption that comes through consumption.

A politics of wellbeing

The critique of modern consumerism and the marketing society set out in this book suggests an alternative political philosophy, one that transcends the mania for maximising economic growth and freeing the market, no matter the cost. We know that above a certain threshold more income does not mean more happiness, yet our entire political and social structure is oriented towards a single goal: maximising the rate of GDP growth. The book argues that growth fetishism and affluenza can cause severe damage to some of the things that really do affect our wellbeing—our health, our personal relationships, our communities, and the natural environment. GDP growth has virtually no relationship with improvements in national wellbeing, and one of the first demands of an alternative political philosopher would be to identify the things that matter and insist that government policies promote them.

What is needed is a political philosophy of wellbeing, one that focuses on those aspects of our personal lives and the social structure that do improve our welfare. A political manifesto for wellbeing is included at the end of this book. The philosophy it promotes would give priority to fulfilling work and help us reclaim our time. It would encourage vibrant, resilient, sustainable communities and help people develop the skills to build stronger family relationships. A politics of wellbeing would wind back the process of commercialising our educational institutions and insist that our schools and universities be devoted to improving the physical, emotional and moral health of our young people, rather than certifying them for the workplace. It would not hesitate to protect us from the forces that spread affluenza, especially the barrage of deceptive marketing. It would recognise when the values of the market intrude into areas of life where they do not belong and—deaf to the self-interested cries for 'choice', 'development' and 'economic freedom'—take measures to exclude them. And we would no longer be tempted to sacrifice the natural world to lift GDP by half a per cent.

Some people have become so habituated to the ideology of the market they have forgotten the lessons of history: 'What you propose is all very well,' they will say, 'but it can never happen. The forces working against it, including human nature, will prevent it'. The argument that there is no stopping the market ideology is antidemocratic because it insists there are forces that will always overwhelm the preferences of the citizenry and that it is pointless for us to collectively pursue a better society.

These are the voices that said the Shah of Iran would never be deposed, that the forces of apartheid were too powerful to be overthrown, and that the Iron Curtain could never be breached. For people who can imagine nothing more than the present, history has ended. If they are right, the future is one in which we accumulate more and more stuff and watch as all aspects of our personal lives and social worlds are turned over to the market.

This dystopian future will be marked by an intensification of all the distress and damage caused by affluenza—unthinking consumerism, fractured relationships, psychological disorders, and mountains of waste. And our children and grandchildren will be condemned to lives without meaning. We believe the people of Australia will not accept such a future.

ENDNOTES

CHAPTER 1

1   *Affluenza*, <www.affluenza.org> [23 December 2004]. Definition modified.

2   The term was popularised in the United States by the KCTS/Seattle and Oregon Public Broadcasting documentary, *Affluenza* (1997, <http://www.pbs.org/kcts/affluenza/show/about.html> [12 January 2005]). One of the producers, John De Graaf, subsequently wrote a book using the term as its title—see John De Graaf, David Wann and Thomas H. Naylor, *Affluenza: the all-consuming epidemic*, Berrett-Koehler Publishers Inc., San Fransisco, 2001.

3   Juliet Schor, *The Overspent American*, HarperCollins, New York, 1998, Table 1.4.

4   P. Saunders, C. Thomson and C. Evans, *Social Change and Social Policy: results from a national survey of public opinion*, Discussion paper no. 106, Social Policy Research Centre, University of New South Wales, Sydney, 2000, p. 19.

5   Robert Frank, *Luxury Fever: money and happiness in an era of excess*, Princeton University Press, New Jersey, 1999, p. 18.

6   Kate Betts, 'Luxury fever: how long will it last?', *Time Magazine*, 'Style and design supplement', Fall, 2004, p. 44.

7   Economists have developed the concept of 'prestige goods'—also known as 'positional goods'—the possession of which signals status. Such goods serve their function only as long as they are unavailable to others.

8   *Good Weekend*, 30–31 October 2004.

9   'Perspective', *Australian Financial Review*, 20–21 November 2004, p. 20.

10 HSBC website, <www.hsbc.com.au/personal/cards/platinum> [11 January 2005].

11 American Express website, <www.americanexpress.com/australia/personal/cards/benefits/platinum_lifestyle.shtml> [11 January 2005].

12 Denis Orrock, cited in B. Brown, 'Credit cards with bells and whistles allow consumers to tap into a wealth of opportunity', *The Australian*, 30 June 2004.

13 Brown, op. cit.

14. <www.frequentflyer.com.au/discuss/viewtopic.php?p=2651> [11 January 2005].

15 See Alain de Botton, *Status Anxiety*, Penguin, London, 2004.

16 See especially Helga Dittmar, 'The role of self-image in excessive buying' in April Lane Benson (ed.), *I Shop, Therefore I Am: compulsive buying and the search for self*, Rowman & Littlefield, Lanham MD, 2000, pp. 105–32.

17 Quoted by Betts, op. cit., p. 30.

18 Tim Kasser, *The High Price of Materialism*, MIT Press, Cambridge MA, 2002, pp. 42, 59, 72.

19 See Richard Eckersley, *Well and Good: how we feel and why it matters*, Text Publishing, Melbourne, 2004, p. 86.

20 For a deeper discussion, see Clive Hamilton, *The Disappointment of Liberalism and the Quest for Inner Freedom*, Discussion paper no. 70, The Australia Institute, Canberra, 2004.

21 See April Lane Benson, op. cit.; Morris Holbrook, Review of *I Shop, Therefore I Am*, in *Psychology and Marketing*, vol. 18, no. 9, September 2001.

22 L. Koran, K. Outlock, J. Hartson, M. Elliot and V. D'Andrea, 'Citalopram treatment of compulsive shopping: an open-label study', *Journal of Clinical Psychiatry, The Primary Care Companion*, vol. 63, 2002, pp. 704–8.

CHAPTER 2

1 Quoted by Betts, op. cit., p. 9.

2 Clive Hamilton, *Overconsumption in Australia: the rise of the middle-class battler*, Discussion paper no. 49, The Australia Institute, Canberra, 2002.

3 Australian Bureau of Statistics, *Australian Social Trends*, Cat. no. 4101.0, ABS, Canberra, 2002.

4 From the 'Amazing homes' supplement, *House & Garden*, October 2004.

5 ibid.

6 ibid.

7 Quoted by Caroline Overington, 'A diamond beats a pair of hearts', *The Age*, 5 January 2004.

8 Figures and quotations in this section are drawn from two Euromonitor reports: 'Pet food and pet care products in Australia' (February 2004), and 'The world market for pet food and pet care products' (April 2004),
<http://www.swin.edu.au/lib/database/euromonitor.htm>
[3 January 2005].

9 About $1.5 billion in official foreign aid plus $358 million donated to overseas aid agencies by private citizens—see AusAID 2004, 'About Australia's overseas aid program',
<http://www.ausaid.gov.au/makediff/whatis.cfm> [3 January 2005] and R. Tomar, *Redefining NGOs: the emerging debate*, Current Issues Brief no. 5, Parliamentary Library, Canberra, 2004.

10 Dominique Jackson, 'Growing up in style', *The Australian*, 19 November 2004, p. 15.

11   Quoted in *The Mercury*, 12 May 2004.
12   *The Age*, 1 August 2004.
13   *Sydney Morning Herald*, 24 June 2004.

CHAPTER 3

1   Coles Myer supplementary response to the Productivity Commission's Inquiry into Textile, Clothing & Footwear Assistance, <http://www.pc.gov.au/inquiry/tcf/subs/subpp143.pdf> [11 January 2005].

2   Robert Vickery, Viclabs, cited on *Today Tonight*, 28 October 2003, <http://seven.com.au/todaytonight/story/?id=14570> [11 January 2005].

3   *Sydney Morning Herald*, 12 September 1994.

4   G. Dixon, 'Kevin Roberts', *New Zealand Listener*, vol. 1931-7, no. 3338, May 2004, <http://www.listener.co.nz/default,1851.sm> [12 January 2005].

5   S. Iyengar and W. Jiang, *Choosing not to Choose: the effects of more choices on retirement savings decisions*, 2004, <http://www.psych.upenn.edu/~baron/choice.overload.pdf> [12 January 2005].

6   Joel S. Dubow (former communications research manager for Coca-Cola), cited in E. Clark, *The Want Makers*, Coronet Books, London, 1988, p. 90.

7   S.M. McClure, J. Li, D. Tomlin, K. Cypert, L. Montague and P. Montague, 'Neural correlates of behavioral preference for culturally familiar drinks', *Neuron*, vol. 44, October 2004, pp. 379–87.

8   H. Tipper, H.L. Holingworth, G.B. Hotchkiss and F.A. Parsons, *Advertising: its principles and practice*, Ronald Press, New York, 1919, cited in E. Clark, op. cit., p. 92.

9   K. Bradsher, *High and Mighty*, PublicAffairs, New York, 2002.

10   K. Braun, R. Ellis and E. Loftus, 'Make my memory: how advertising can change our memories of the past', *Psychology and Marketing*, vol. 19, no. 1, 2002, pp. 1–23.

11 Juliet Schor, *Born to Buy*, Scribner, New York, 2004.

12 ibid., p. 23.

13 Anne Adriance (former head of kids' business at Saatchi and Saatchi), cited in T.L. Stanley, 'Kiddie cars', *Brandweek*, 23 October 1995, pp. 38–40.

14 Brad Boeckmann, cited in Stanley, ibid.

15 Schor, op. cit., p. 24.

16 Australian Association of National Advertisers, Code for Advertising to Children.

17 Kellog 2004, 'Tell me more about Coco Pops', *Kellog*, <www.kellogg.com.au/DisplayPage.asp?PageID=483&brandid=5> [11 January 2005].

18 <www.kellogs.com.au/NutritionInfo/> [11 January 2005].

19 Percentages for food advertising to children are based on the number of junk food ads seen by a child watching four hours of television a day over a six-week holiday period. In this period they would see 649 junk food ads, including 404 for fast food, 135 for soft drinks and 44 for ice-cream products—Australian Divisions of General Practice, *What are We Feeding our Children? A Junk Food Advertising Audit*, National Divisions Youth Alliance, ADGP, Canberra, 2003.

20 ibid.

21 Nancy Shalek (president of Shalek Advertising), cited in G. Ruskin, 'Why they whine: how corporations prey on our children', *Mothering*, issue 97, 1999, p. 42, <http://www.siop.org/tip/backissues/TipJuly00/34Kanner.htm> [11 January 2005].

22 Cited in G. Ruskin, ibid.

23 C. Teague Jnr., *Research Planning Memorandum on Some Thoughts about New Brands of Cigarettes for the Youth Market*, 2 February 1973, cited in Action on Smoking and Health, *Marketing to Children*, *Action on Smoking and Health*, <www.ash.org.uk/html/conduct/html/tobexpld3.html#References> [11 January 2005].

24 Cited in Sarah Schmidt, 'Branded babies: marketing turns tots into logo-conscious consumers', *CanWest News Service*, 6 May 2003.

25 Cited in ibid.

26 Cheryl Idell, *The Nag Factor*, report commissioned by Western International Media, Los Angeles, 1998.

27 Cited in Juliet Schor, op. cit., p. 62.

28 A. Kanner and T. Kasser, 'Stuffing our kids: should psychologists help advertisers manipulate children?', *Society for Industrial and Organisational Psychology*, 2000, <www.siop.org/tip/backissues/TipJuly00/34Kanner.htm> [11 January 2005].

29 Martin Lindstrom, *BrandChild: remarkable insights into the minds of today's global kids and their relationship with brands*, Kogan Page, London, 2003, p. 46.

30 ibid., p. 77.

31 ibid., pp. 6, 23.

32 ibid., p. 82.

33 ibid., p. 196.

CHAPTER 4

1 See, for example, Bruno Frey and Alois Stutzer, *Happiness and Economics*, Princeton University Press, Princeton NJ, 2002, p. 91.

2 Justine McNamara, Rachel Lloyd, Matthew Toohey and Anne Harding, *Prosperity for All? How Low Income Families Have Fared in the Boom Times*, National Centre for Social and Economic Modelling, University of Canberra, 2004. The average disposable income for the poorest 20 per cent of families was $28 800 a year. This group is dominated by welfare recipients and includes a disproportionate share of single parents.

3 Hamilton, *Overconsumption in Australia*, op. cit.

4 Holbrook, op. cit.

5 Clive Hamilton, *Overconsumption in Britain: a culture of middle-class complaint?*, Discussion paper no. 57, The Australia Institute, Canberra,

2003. GDP is measured by purchasing power parity—that is, taking account of differences in exchange rates and differences in the purchasing power of domestic currencies in each country.

6 Strictly speaking, equivalised household incomes would be better, that is, incomes adjusted for household size.

7 It should be noted that the US survey was conducted in 1995 and the results might differ if it were repeated today. There has been a decade of luxury fever since that time, so it would be reasonable to assume that more Americans feel that their incomes are inadequate.

8 Frey and Stutzer, op. cit., p. 9.

9 Rob Bray, *Hardship in Australia: an analysis of financial stress indicators in the 1998–99 Australian Bureau of Statistics Household Expenditure Survey*, Occasional paper no. 4, Department of Family and Community Services, Canberra, 2002.

10 Reported by Bray, ibid.

11 ibid., p. 17.

CHAPTER 5

1 Reserve Bank of Australia, 'Household debt: what the data show', *Reserve Bank of Australia Bulletin*, RBA, Sydney, March 2003, Table 1.

2 National Centre for Social and Economic Modelling, 'Household debt in Australia—walking the tightrope', *AMP.NATSEM Income and Wealth Report*, issue 9, NATSEM, Canberra, November 2004, Table 8.

3 Inspector-General in Bankruptcy, *Annual Report, 2003–2004*, Insolvency and Trustee Service of Australia, Canberra, 2004.

4 Dun and Bradstreet, 'D&B expands call centre capacity with Datacom to meet growth in debt business', 9 July 2002, <www.dnb.com/about/media/press/> [11 January 2005].

5 Insolvency and Trustee Service of Australia, Annual reports, various issues, ITSA, Canberra.

6 Paul Brennan (Citigroup), cited in Matt Wade, 'Exports a chink in Howard's economic armour', *Sydney Morning Herald*, 3 September 2004.

7   Don Harding, Matt Hammill, Anne Leahy and Peter Summers, *ING – Melbourne Institute Household Saving Report*, Melbourne Institute of Applied Economic and Social Research, University of Melbourne, June quarter 2001, pp. 6–7.

8   National Centre for Social and Economic Modelling, op. cit., Figure 12. About 38 per cent of households in this income range have credit card debts, while only 16 per cent of households with incomes less than $20 000 have them.

9   Reserve Bank of Australia, op. cit., Table 1.

10 Catherine Wolthuizen (Australian Consumers' Association), cited in R. Myer and S. Dabkowski, 'The never-never is gaining on us', *The Age*, 9 June 2002.

11 National Centre for Social and Economic Modelling, op. cit., p. 11.

12 See, for example, Gary Jones, 'Don't use credit cards says Barclaycard boss', *Daily Mirror* (London), 17 October 2003.

13 National Centre for Social and Economic Modelling, op. cit., p. 11.

14 Wide Bay Australia Ltd 2004, 'Home loans', *Products and Services*, <www.widebaycap.com.au> [8 January 2005].

15 GE Loans 2004, <www.geloans.com.au/equity.html> [20 December 2004].

16 Australian Bureau of Statistics, *Australian National Accounts: national income, expenditure and product*, Cat. no. 5206.0, ABS, Canberra, 2004, Table 3.

17 Between 1990 and 2004 imports of consumption goods grew by 263 per cent compared with capital goods growth of 164 per cent and growth in intermediate goods of 135 per cent—Australian Bureau of Statistics, *International Merchandise Imports, Australia*, Cat. no. 5439.0, ABS, Canberra, 2004, Table 8.

CHAPTER 6

1   Rodney Tiffen and Ross Gittins, *How Australia Compares*, Cambridge University Press, Cambridge, 2004, Table 4.25.

2   ibid., Table 4.19.

3 Australian Bureau of Statistics, *Labour Force Australia, 2003*, Cat. no. 6203.0, ABS, Canberra, July 2004.

4 Australian Bureau of Statistics, *Labour Force Australia*, Cat. no. 6291.0, ABS, Canberra, December 2003.

5 ibid.

6 M. Wooden, 'Industrial relations reform and the consequences for working time, job security, productivity and jobs', Paper presented to the Towards Opportunity and Prosperity Conference, Melbourne, 4–5 April 2002, <www1.ecom.unimelb.edu.au/iaesrwww/conf/top2002/pdffiles/WoodenMark.pdf> [11 January 2005].

7 R. Denniss, *Annual Leave in Australia: an analysis of entitlements, usage and preferences*, Discussion paper no. 56, The Australia Institute, Canberra, 2003.

8 ibid.

9 D. MacDonald, I. Campbell and J. Burgess, 'Ten years of enterprise bargaining in Australia: an introduction', *Labour and Industry*, vol. 12, August 2001, p. 1.

10 C. Hamilton, *Carpe Diem? The Deferred Happiness Syndrome*, Webpaper, The Australia Institute, Canberra, May 2004.

11 Mike Steketee, 'Hearts say stay, but heads say work', *The Australian*, 1 November 2001.

12 J. Dagge, 'My career-stressed wives' club', *Sun-Herald*, 15 September 2002.

13 C. Breakspear and C. Hamilton, *Getting a Life: understanding the downshifting phenomenon in Australia*, Discussion paper no. 62, The Australia Institute, Canberra, February 2004.

14 Hamilton, *Carpe Diem?*, op. cit.

15 T. Uehata, 'Long working hours and occupational stress related cardiovascular attacks among middle aged workers in Japan', *Journal of Human Ergology*, vol. 20, 2001, pp. 147–53.

16 D. Dawson, K. McCulloch and A. Baker, *Extended Working Hours in Australia*, Report commissioned by the Department of Industrial

Relations, Centre for Sleep Research, University of South Australia, Adelaide, 2001.

17 ibid., p. 14.

18 F. Nachreiner, S. Akkermann and K. Haenecke, 'Fatal accident risk as a function of hours into work', cited in Dawson et al., op. cit.

19 S. Bent, 'The psychological effects of extended working hours' in Kathryn Heiler (ed.), *The Twelve Hour Workday: emerging issues*, Working paper no. 51, Australian Centre for Industrial Relations Research and Training, Sydney, 1998, p. 26.

20 See ibid.; Dawson et al., op. cit; and M. Hatch, B. Ji, X. Sho and M. Susser, 'Do standing, lifting, climbing or long hours during pregnancy have an effect on foetal growth?', *Epidemiology*, vol. 8, no. 5, 1997, pp. 530–6.

21 Paul McFedries 2000, 'Presenteeism', *The Word Spy*, <www.wordspy.com/words/presenteeism.asp> [11 January 2005].

22 Barbara Pocock, *The Work/Life Collision*, The Federation Press, Sydney, 2003, p. 159.

23 ibid., p. 94.

24 ibid., p. 29.

25 R. Eckerlsey, *Quality of Life in Australia: an analysis of public perceptions*, Discussion paper no. 23, The Australia Institute, Canberra, 1999.

26 Pocock, op. cit., p. 110.

27 Barbara Pocock and Jane Clarke, *Can't Buy Me Love? Young Australians' Views on Parental Work, Time, Guilt and Their Own Consumption*, Discussion paper no. 61, The Australia Institute, Canberra, 2004.

28 ibid.

29 ibid., p. 17.

CHAPTER 7

1 Ross Honeywell, cited by Alex May, 'Consumption therapy', *Sydney Morning Herald*, 22 December 2004.

2   Marcus Walker, 'Europe walks a tightrope', *Australian Financial Review*, 15 December 2004, p. 52.

3   ibid.

4   Which makes it all the more puzzling that Ian Kiernan, head of Clean Up Australia, has taken a strong public stance against what would perhaps be the most effective measure to cut plastic waste in Australia—a compulsory levy on plastic bags. ABC TV's *Four Corners* program revealed in September 2003 that Clean Up Australia's Bag Yourself a Better Environment program, which called for greater voluntary efforts, was sponsored by Coles and Woolworths.

5   Unless otherwise indicated, all the data in this chapter are drawn from survey results reported in C. Hamilton, R. Denniss and D. Baker, *Wasteful Consumption in Australia*, Discussion paper no. 77, The Australia Institute, Canberra, 2005. The survey, with 1644 respondents, was carried out by Roy Morgan Research in November–December 2004.

6   As suggested later, the estimate of wasteful spending is likely to be too low and we could probably clear our credit cards in one year.

7   George Wilkenfeld, 'Energy efficiency programs in the residential sector', in W.J. Bouma, G.I. Pearman and M.R. Manning (eds), *Greenhouse: coping with climate change*, CSIRO Publishing, Melbourne, 1996, Table 1.

8   Hamilton, Denniss and Baker, *Wasteful Consumption*, op. cit.

9   OECD, Selected environmental data, <www.oecd.org/dataoecd/11/15/24111692.PDF> [11 January 2005].

10 BDA Group 2003, *The Potential of Market Based Instruments to Better Manage Australia's Waste Streams*, <www.deh.gov.au/industry/waste/mbi/pubs/study.pdf> [11 January 2005].

11 State of the Environment Advisory Council, *Australia: state of the environment report 2001*, CSIRO Publishing Melbourne, 2002.

12 US Department of Agriculture 2004, *A Citizen's Guide to Food Recovery*, <www.usda.gov/news/pubs/gleaning/two.htm> [11 January 2005].

13 Prudential Insurance, *Soggy Lettuce Report 2004*, Prudential Insurance, London, 2004.

CHAPTER 8

1 Martin Seligman, 'Why is there so much depression today? The waxing of the individual and the waning of the commons', in Rick Ingram (ed.), *Contemporary Psychological Approaches to Depression*, Plenum Press, New York, 1990.

2 *The Guardian*, 8 November 2003, p. 2.

3 Office of National Statistics, *Psychiatric Morbidity among Adults*, Technical report, ONS, London, 2000.

4 C. Murray and A. Lopez (eds), *The Global Burden of Disease: summary*, WHO & World Bank, Geneva, 1996, p. 21.

5 The following discussion draws on C. Hamilton, *Comfortable, Relaxed and Drugged to the Eye-balls*, Webpaper, The Australia Institute, Canberra, June 2003.

6 Using the Kessler Psychological Distress Scale, a scale based on ten questions about negative emotional states in the four weeks preceding the interview.

7 Australian Bureau of Statistics, *National Health Survey*, Cat. no. 4364.0, ABS, Canberra, 2002.

8 Australian Institute of Health and Welfare, *2001 National Drug Strategy Household Survey: first results*, AIHW, Canberra, 2002, p. 18.

9 *Herald-Sun*, 12 November 2002, p. 15.

10 Australian Institute of Health and Welfare, op. cit., p. 36.

11 Tim Kasser, *The High Price of Materialism*, MIT Press, Cambridge MA, 2002, p. 22.

12 R. Moynihan, I. Heath, D. Henry and P. Gotzsche, 'Selling sickness:

the pharmaceutical industry and disease mongering', *British Medical Journal,* vol. 324, issue 7342, April 2002, pp. 886–91.

13   Ray Moynihan, 'The making of a disease: female sexual dysfunction', *British Medical Journal,* vol. 326, issue 7379, 4 January 2003, pp. 45–7.

14   Moynihan et al., op. cit.

15   The following is based on Moynihan et al., op. cit.

16   R. Moynihan et al., op. cit., p. 886.

17   B. Mintzes, 'For and against: direct to consumer advertising is medicalising normal human experience', *British Medical Journal,* vol. 324, issue 7342, 13 April 2002, p. 908.

18   Moynihan et al., op. cit., pp. 886–91.

19   ibid., p. 888.

20   J. Avorn, M. Chen and R. Hartley, 'Scientific versus commercial sources of influence on the prescribing behavior of physicians', *American Journal of Medicine,* vol. 73, 1982, pp. 4–8.

21   I. Kawachi and P. Conrad, 'Medicalization and the pharmacological treatment of blood pressure' in P. Davis (ed.), *Contested Ground: public purpose and private interests in the regulation of prescription drugs,* Oxford University Press, New York, 1996.

22   J. Baird, 'Self-mutilation or beauty—it's only a fine line', *Sydney Morning Herald,* 22 July 2002.

23   R. Finnila, 'Nips and tucks a snip on gift lists', *Courier-Mail,* 30 November 2004.

24   S. Stock, 'Yuletide turns to nip, tuck and suck', *The Australian,* 16 December 2000.

25   ibid. The former head of a New South Wales government inquiry into plastic surgery, Professor Merrilyn Walton, said that she was opposed to plastic surgery gifts because they put recipients in a vulnerable position: 'The obligations on the recipient are quite powerful and it does not place them in an independent mind frame . . . The person may feel pressured to accept the gift and it could erode already low self-esteem'—quoted by Stock, ibid.

26 *Entertainment Tonight*,
    <www.entertainmenttonight.com/celebrity/a15483.htm>
    [3 July 2003].
27 *ABC News in Science*, <www.abc.net.au/science/news> [17 June 2002].
28 *ABC News in Science*, <www.abc.net.au/science/news>
    [11 March 2003].

CHAPTER 9

1   *Canberra Times*, 6 August 2002.
2   *Sydney Morning Herald*, 12 August 2002.
3   John Stuart Mill, *Principles of Political Economy*, 6th edn, Longmans,
    Green and Co., London, 1923, pp. 748–9.
4   See the newsletter of financial planners Lifestyle Online,
    <www.lifestyleonline.com.au> [12 January 2005].
5   Quoted by Barbara Pocock and Jane Clark, *Can't Buy Me Love*, Dis-
    cussion paper no. 61, The Australia Institute, Canberra, 2004.
6   The Harwood Group, *Yearning for Balance: views of Americans on
    consumption, materialism, and the environment*, Report prepared for
    the Merck Family Fund, 1995, <www.iisd.ca/linkages/consume/
    harwood.html> [11 January 2005].
7   Richard Eckersley, *Quality of Life in Australia: an analysis of public
    perceptions*, Discussion paper no. 23, The Australia Institute,
    Canberra, 1999.
8   C. Hamilton, *Overconsumption*, op. cit.
9   Michael Flood and Clive Hamilton, *Regulating Youth Access to
    Pornography*, Discussion paper no. 53, The Australia Institute,
    March 2003.
10 Lisa Ryan and Suzanne Dziurawiec, 'Materialism and its relation-
    ship to life satisfaction', *Social Indicators Research*, vol. 55, issue 2,
    August 2001, p. 185.

CHAPTER 10

1   See Clive Hamilton and Elizabeth Mail, *Downshifting in Australia: a sea-change in the pursuit of happiness*, Discussion paper no. 50, The Australia Institute, Canberra, 2003. Those who 'downshifted' by refusing a promotion, stopping work to start their own businesses, going back to study or stopping work to look after a baby were excluded because their motives are unclear.

2   Clive Hamilton, *Downshifting in Britain: a sea-change in the pursuit of happiness*, Discussion paper no. 58, The Australia Institute, Canberra, 2003.

3· C. Breakspear and C. Hamilton, op. cit. The names of the people interviewed have been changed to protect their privacy.

CHAPTER 11

1   Lambesis Agency 2004, *L Style Report*, 9th edn, <http://www.lstylereport.com> [11 January 2005].

INDEX

A political manifesto for wellbeing

Preamble

Australians are three times richer than their parents and grand-parents were in the 1950s, but they are not happier. Despite the evidence of a declino in national wellbeing, governments continue to put the interests of the economy first. Our obsession with economic growth and money means other things that could improve our well-being are sacrificed.

In the community there is a widespread belief that the values of the market—individualism, selfishness, materialism, competition—are driving out the more desirable values of trust, self-restraint, mutual respect and generosity.

Despite this anxiety, most people today feel alienated from the political process. The main parties seem too alike and have given up trying to build a better society.

The challenge of our age is to build a new politics that is committed, above all, to improving our wellbeing.

Wellbeing

We often think of wellbeing as happiness, but it is more than that. It is also about having meaning in our lives, about developing as a person and feeling that our lives are fulfilling and worthwhile.

Our wellbeing is shaped by our genes, our upbringing, our personal circumstances and choices, and the social conditions we live in. Our collective wellbeing is improved if we live in a peaceful, flourishing, supportive society. Promoting wellbeing should be a political as well as a personal task.

Wellbeing comes from having a web of relationships and interests. Family and friends, work, leisure activities and spiritual beliefs can all increase our wellbeing. The intimacy, the sense of belonging and the support offered by close personal relationships are of greatest importance. Having more money matters most to the poor and to people who lack other sources of wellbeing, but for most Australians it counts little towards improving wellbeing.

Throughout history sages have counselled that happiness is not a goal but rather a consequence of how we live and that it comes from being content with what we have. Today, we are sold a different message—that we will be happy only if we have more money and more of the things money buys. Human experience and scientific research does not support this belief.

What can governments do?

Governments can't legislate to make us happy, but many things they do affect our wellbeing. With time, they can change for good or ill the society and culture we live in. Industrial relations laws damage or improve the quality of our working lives; government policies protect or defile the environment; our children's education depends on the quality of schools; tax policies can make the difference between a fair and an unfair society; the cohesiveness of our communities is affected by city design and transport plans.

This manifesto proposes eight areas in which a government could enact policies to improve national wellbeing.

---

1. Measure what matters

Economic growth is treated as the panacea for all our social ills. But growth in GDP has almost no connection with improvements in national wellbeing. Bushfires, car accidents and crime waves all increase GDP, but they don't make us better off. GDP takes no account of how increases in income are distributed or of the damage to the natural environment that economic activity can cause.

We need a set of national wellbeing accounts so that we can monitor our progress. These accounts should report on the quality of work, the state of our communities, our health, the strength of our relationships, and the state of the environment. Governments should be judged by how much our wellbeing improves—not by how much the economy expands.

---

2. Provide fulfilling work

Fulfilling work is vital to our wellbeing; insecure, stressful and unsatisfying jobs diminish it. High-quality work can provide us with purpose, challenge and opportunities. Through it we can develop our capacities, begin to realise our potential, and meet many of our social needs. In short, fulfilling work is essential if we are to flourish. Workplaces that provide secure, rewarding jobs should be encouraged. Workplace flexibility, including quality part-time jobs, should operate in the interests of employees as well as employers.

Unemployment is more damaging than just the loss of income, and disparaging unemployed people serves only to increase their anxiety and sense of exclusion. Pursuing full employment is essential to a wellbeing economy, as is ensuring decent minimum workplace standards.

Satisfying work can be found inside and outside the home. Work in the household is essential to the health and wellbeing of families and communities but, because it is outside the economy, it is ignored. Governments should value this work, and employers need to adapt to the realities of family life. Maternity leave, paternity leave, carers' leave and sick leave are not costs to be avoided: they are rights.

---

3. Reclaim our time

Among the countries of the developed world, Australians now work the longest hours and have less holiday leave than most. We systematically overestimate the amount of wellbeing associated with high incomes and long work hours. Our families, our health and our sense of achievement all suffer from this miscalculation.

If Australia is to thrive, our working lives should contribute to, rather than sap, our wellbeing and that of our families. Spending more time with our families, friends and communities would make most of us happier, and our workplaces must be reshaped to allow us to reclaim our time.

To flourish as a nation, not just as an economy, we need to limit working hours by reducing the maximum working week to 35 hours during the next eight to ten years and by more thereafter. Other developed counties have introduced reduced working hours without the often-predicted chaos. If we took productivity gains in the form of a shorter working week rather than higher pay we could improve our quality of life and create new job opportunities, all without any reduction in pay.

4. Rethink education

It is impossible for all students to come first in their class, and our education system should stop pretending they can. Educators should aim to give all children rich lives, rather than training them to win the rat race. Our schools should be dedicated to creating capable, confident, emotionally mature young people who are equipped to face life's vicissitudes.

Young Australians are told they will have up to six careers in their lifetime, yet we insist on making schools and universities more vocationally oriented. As a result, students learn less about themselves and the societies around them. A greater focus on children's physical, emotional and moral wellbeing—rather than competitive test results—would produce happier, healthier young people who are better able to understand themselves and their communities.

We should stop turning universities into businesses selling degrees and instead concentrate on making them places where students flourish as humans and academics feel free to question powerful institutions without fear of victimisation.

5. Invest in early childhood

Studies show that, for each dollar wisely invested in early childhood education and care, we can save up to seven dollars in avoided costs of crime, unemployment, remedial education and welfare payments.

Children need a great deal of individual attention in their early years, preferably from their parents. Shared parental leave should be extended to cover the first two years of a child's life. Parents, too, need support so they can do the best job for their children.

---

6. Discourage materialism and promote responsible advertising

Buying a particular brand of margarine cannot give us a happy family, and owning a 4WD will not deliver us from humdrum lives. But the advertisers know they can persuade us otherwise. Advertising makes us more materialistic, even though we know that people who are more materialistic are more self-absorbed, less community oriented and less happy. Materialism is also bad for the environment.

Marketers have hijacked the media and most of our cultural events, and it is impossible to escape their daily barrage. We need commercial-free zones in our cities and limits on shopping developments. And governments should use tax and retirement policies to help people who want to change to a less materialistic lifestyle.

Advertisers prey especially on children because they know children lack the critical capacity to distinguish between facts and advertising fiction. As in Sweden, advertising to children aged less than twelve years should be banned, and advertising codes of conduct should be legislated so that irresponsible and deceptive marketing is outlawed.

7. Protect the environment

A healthy, diverse natural environment is valuable in itself; it is also essential to our wellbeing. But government and business tell us we cannot afford too much protection, that it is bad for GDP. We know, though, that the wellbeing of future generations will be severely affected if we fail to resolutely tackle climate change, loss of bio-diversity, pollution and waste.

We can do much more than we have done to date. We should move towards a system that increases taxes on damaging environmental activities such as burning fossil fuels and reduces taxes on socially beneficial activities such as providing fulfilling work. We should make the generation of waste very expensive and reward businesses and households that reduce their consumption and recycle materials.

---

8. Build communities and relationships

A flourishing society is characterised by vibrant, resilient, sustainable communities. Loneliness and isolation cause much unhappiness, especially among unemployed people, older people living alone and people with disabilities.

Instead of criticising single parents who do the best they can, we should support them. Instead of judging people by their sexuality, we should encourage all loving and supportive relationships. And we need to help people develop the skills to build stronger family relationships.

We all depend on others for care at some time in our lives. Care is provided by parents, children, friends and others. We need to value all carers more. Governments and employers should do much more to support workers with caring responsibilities.

Governments should support engagement in community

organisations, especially among marginalised groups. Volunteers contribute greatly to our wellbeing and need to be recognised and rewarded.

Towards a flourishing society

The question for Australia in the twenty-first century is not how we can become richer: it is how we can use our high standard of living to build a flourishing society—one devoted to improving our wellbeing rather than just expanding the economy.

Australians are anxious about declining moral standards. We worry that we have become too selfish, materialistic and superficial and long for a society built on mutual respect, self-restraint and generosity of spirit.

The changes proposed in this manifesto would inspire better communities, stronger personal relationships, happier workplaces, a better balance between work and home, less commercialisation, and greater environmental protection.

A flourishing society is not a futile hope. Australian democracy offers people the opportunity to shed their cynicism and start building a better future.

Visit <www.wellbeingmanifesto.net> and endorse this manifesto.

Clive Hamilton, Richard Denniss and Richard Eckersley prepared this manifesto. They acknowledge the New Economics Foundation in London for permission to draw heavily on its manifesto.